Surgery for the Soul

BRENDA L. CALDWELL, PH. D.

BRENDA L. CALDWELL., PH. D.

Copyright © 2017 Brenda L. Caldwell, Ph.D.

All Rights Reserved

ISBN-10:

0692971858

ISBN-13: 978-0692971857 (Unlimited Life Publishing)

DEDICATION

I dedicate this book to the memory and legacy of my beloved great-nephew Steven, whose tragic death gave birth to a profound purpose. Countless wounded souls have been healed through the story of his brief but impactful life! I also dedicate this book to the memory of beloved first grade teacher, Mrs. Pentecost, who made an empowering impact on my life. God used her to alter the course of my life and I am forever grateful.

BRENDA L. CALDWELL., PH. D.

SURGERY FOR THE SOUL

CONTENTS

	Acknowledgments	7
	Introduction	9
1	Facing Your "Uns"	11
2	Who Cracked Your Mirror?	35
3	Bruised, Broken, and Bitter	57
4	The Unforgiving Heart	73
5	Choose to Forgive/Choose to Live	91
6	The Surgery: New Heart for a New Start	107
7	God's Favor Follows Forgiveness	123
8	I Love What I See When I Look at Me	135
	About the Author	

BRENDA L. CALDWELL., PH. D.

ACKNOWLEDGEMENTS

First and foremost, with the help of the Holy Spirit, I am grateful to finally write this special book that was in my spirit for over ten years! To God be the glory for what he ordained this book to do on the earth.

I also want to thank some special people in my life who have supported me from the beginning to the end of this project. To my mother, Ruth Parker and my sister, Lisa Parker, thanks for believing in me and giving me words of encouragement. To my *Paragon Team*, A., A.G., and C.O., thank you for holding me accountable to my dreams! To my awesome editing teams, Kelsy Jelinek (lead editor), DeChundra "Dee Dee" Knowles (assistant editor), and Chiquita Mcghee (cover design), thanks for doing an amazing job preparing this book for my readers. Dee Dee, thanks so much for being my daily Barnabas all these years!

To my *WOW Sisters*, words cannot fully express my deep appreciation for each of you for your labor of love and support! To my Barbados family, Anderson and Shamelle Rice, thank you for receiving me into your home and your hearts during our ministry partnership with Jabez House. I am so grateful God connected us. To Lanita Smith, your obedience revolutionized my thinking. Thank you! I give special thanks to Tamika Mitchell, my former Bridges student, who for over five years constantly asked, "Dr. B, when is your next book coming out? I'm ready for it!" God truly used you! To my family and dear friends, thank you so much for believing in my work! I appreciate all of you beyond words!

BRENDA L. CALDWELL., PH. D.

INTRODUCTION

It seems like people are angrier now more than ever! It has sadly become the norm to hear of mass shootings, domestic violence, road rage assaults, bullying, violence against law enforcement, and other acts of violence as acceptable realities in our society. This should never be acceptable, but every problem has a root. Happy people don't hurt people. Healed people don't hurt people. Hurting people hurt people! I believe the root cause stems from what I call "Uns:" Unhealed hurt, Unresolved issues, and Unmet needs that lead to the biggest "Un" of all, Unforgiveness!

Many times the "Uns" start in childhood and follow us into adulthood where they play out in issues like those mentioned above. Having worked in counseling and ministry for many years, I have met countless souls, emotionally wounded and desiring healing. I felt led to write *Surgery for the Soul: Healing for the Hurting Heart* to shed light on the powerful truth that FORGIVENESS is the surgery that heals the soul. These eleven letters have power to heal broken relationships, broken hearts, broken bodies, and broken homes. Even with this truth, people struggle to walk in true forgiveness (whether forgiving others or receiving forgiveness) due to painful life experiences like abuse, abandonment, rejection, father issues, mother issues, divorce, betrayal, and relationship hurts. Is this you? If so, you're reading the right book at the right time because God wants you to let go of anything hindering you from being who he created you to be.

Surgery for the Soul: Healing for the Hurting Heart was birthed out of a painful experience years ago that produced purpose and passion in my life to help wounded souls and those who have wounded to be set free! I love seeing *hurting* souls *healed* and *wounded* souls walking in their *worth*! With a personal and engaging style, we will journey to a destination called "Mercy Hospital" and experience therapeutic heart surgery similar to receiving a spiritual heart transplant. Along the way, you will "Face Your "Uns," and answer the question "Who Cracked Your Mirror?" You will discover how "Bruised, Broken, and Bitter" you are, learn about "The Unforgiving Heart," and be given an opportunity to "Choose to Forgive" so you can "Choose to Live." Arriving at "Mercy Hospital" for "The Surgery," you will receive insight on how "God's Favor Follows Forgiveness." At the final destination, you will be able to declare, "I Love What I See When I Look at Me." As you turn the page to start this journey, keep two things in mind: God loves you and healing awaits!

1

FACING YOUR "UNS"

It often starts in childhood. A father abandons you. A nice neighbor becomes a monster molester. A band of bullies make school almost unbearable. A mean teacher degrades you, breaking your spirit. A merciless mother beats you for no reason. A best friend spreads a vicious rumor about you. A family member rejects you because you look "different." A church member rapes you one night after bible study. So, what is it that many times starts in childhood and follows you to the grave? "Uns" . . . unhealed hurts, unresolved issues, and unmet needs!

What Kind of Hurts are We Talking about?

Unhealed hurts, or emotional wounds, are hurts that produce painful memories that result from being rejected, abandoned, abused, neglected, embarrassed, shamed, terrorized, scared, manipulated, or otherwise violated. Hurts, wounds, and pain that remain long after the events that caused them, will disrupt our lives.

Calling such hurts "scars" is inappropriate. A scar indicates healing of a wound. The tissue inside a scar is usually stronger than the tissue around it. Unhealed hurts are "open wounds" that continue to fester and flare up. They cause emotional pain, suffering, or sometimes physical discomfort, illness, and serious disruption to daily functioning.

If you've been dealing with such hurts, it is critical for you to understand that your unhealed hurt is spiritually rooted in Satan's plot to "steal, kill, and destroy" your life by any means necessary (John 10:10)! Ever since his eviction from heaven for "seeking to be like the Most High," Satan has opposed God by tormenting his children (Isaiah 14:14). As a child of God who has a purpose and destiny, Satan will use every unhealed hurt in your past to keep you ensnared in a bondage of recurring pain.

Hole in the Soul

The soul is made up of the mind (thoughts and memories), the will (desires), and the emotions (inner spirit or "emotional heart"). Even when hurts have been thoroughly suppressed and no longer infect the conscious memory, they can remain open wounds and affect the quality of your life. Satan is the biggest "crack addict" on earth because he is addicted to searching for cracks in the soul. He sets out to destroy relationships, self-esteem, confidence, health, the ability to give and receive love, and so much more. He doesn't care if you were an innocent, defenseless child when you were first abused. He will take this abuse and torture you with feelings of shame, guilt, self-hate, bitterness, resentment, anger, and rejection for the rest of your life . . . or until the "hole" in your soul is filled with the plug of *forgiveness* (much more on this word is coming later). Most of the time, this hole is filled with vices such as food, alcohol, shopping, busyness, gambling, pornography, sex, or abuse of pain pills, and other drugs. Unfortunately, none of these vices will give solace to a hurting soul.

Third John chapter 2 (KJV) the author declares, "Beloved, I wish above all things that you would prosper and be in health, even as your soul prospers." It is God's perfect will that we would prosper in every area of life . . . mentally, physically, emotionally, financially, socially, and spiritually. This is a recipe for wholeness. However, in 1 Peter 5:8, Satan "roams around like a roaring lion seeking whom he may devour." He wishes above all things that we would perish in the pain of unhealed hurt and remain bound in emotional baggage forever.

Deal with It or Live with It

If allowed to remain, unhealed hurts lead to many problems, some quite serious. For example, depression often results from unreleased or unresolved anger. The anger arises from a particular hurt, which, for various reasons, the suffering person cannot express constructively. Instead, the hurt is pushed deep inside. The truth is that whatever is buried inside does not die. Sometimes depression results from fear and anxiety that is not discussed, but repressed. This leaves a feeling of hopelessness, and what some psychologists describe as having "no control." Sometimes depression leads to suicide or harmful acts towards others, including family members. Some may experience what medical experts call "psychosomatic" illnesses that are physical illnesses with psychological roots. Those with unhealed hurts might withdraw into a shell, while others may exhibit forms of rage or an inability to relate to others in a healthy way. Sometimes those with hurts inflict on others the same acts that produced the hurts in them, particularly in abuse cases. In other words, in many cases, "hurt people, hurt people."

Having a counseling practice for several years, I would say that everyone, to some degree, has experienced past hurts . . . some less serious than others. Everyone can benefit from healing those hurts. As we grow up and suffer various hurts that are not resolved or healed, we become like houses in which the garbage (unresolved, unhealed hurt) is thrown into the basement. After a few years, the entire house begins to stink.

SURGERY FOR THE SOUL

When Unhealed Hurt is Not Confronted!

My motto that I often share with clients whether in one-on-one or group sessions is, *"God can't heal until you get real."* As ugly as it is to face, we have to be willing to *admit* to the problem in order to *heal* from it. Some of these "ugly" unhealed hurts include insecurities, addictions, anger, resentment, bitterness, rejection, hatred, depression, self-hate, an inability to maintain healthy relationships, and a host of other issues. If not confronted, these unhealed hurts will lead to other issues such as anxiety attacks, autoimmune conditions, and similar conditions or diseases. Such problems often arise when people suppress and do not express the emotions they feel while undergoing negative and painful experiences, whether physical, verbal, or psychological. The normal reaction to such experiences is fight or flight, to respond aggressively or to escape. Unfortunately, too many victims do neither. They merely endure the hurts and stuff the emotions into an internal closet. For some people, suffering repeated emotional hurts over a long period will cause the body to react in harmful ways.

When Courage to Confront Kicks In

When we have courage to confront unhealed hurts, we stand on the powerful promise of God's word expressed in Psalm 103:1-5 (NIV),

> "Bless the Lord, O my soul and all that is within me, bless His holy name. Bless the Lord, O my soul, and forget not all his benefits; who forgives all my sins, who heals all my diseases; who redeemed my life from destruction; who crowns me with loving kindness and tender mercies; who satisfies my mouth with good things; so that my youth is renewed like the eagle's."

God promises to heal all that is within you, including your unhealed hurt. However, you must first be willing to confront it. Some of His other benefits include healing all of your sins, healing your diseases, protecting you from the destruction of Satan, and even restoring you to having a carefree, youthful spirit! What an awesome bundle of gifts! This is exactly why Satan, the adversary of your soul, doesn't want you to experience true healing. His scheme is to keep you so bound up in the unhealed hurt that you never walk in the fullness of God's promis

Desperation Can be a Good Thing

The next type of "Un" that must be faced is *unresolved issues*. This happens when one is negatively affected emotionally by a situation that has yet to receive closure. Many times this leaves our souls fragmented. I called this being *broken*, *damaged*, *cracked*, or *chipped*. On some level, we all have or have had something unresolved from our past.

In Luke 8:43-48 (KJV), the bible gives an account of a woman who had "an issue of blood" which she dealt with for twelve years. She went to many doctors, spent all of her money, and still had an unresolved issue that caused an unstoppable hemorrhage. She was drained, destitute, and desperate for help. In one act of desperation, this "unclean" woman broke the religious law of not being allowed to touch a Jewish man, when she pressed her way through a crowd. She touched the cloak of Jesus, to which he responded, "Daughter, your faith has made you whole."

One of the gems in this story is how *desperation* can lead to *deliverance*! This unnamed woman was so tired of living with her unresolved issue that, at all costs, she did what was necessary to receive healing. Now, here's the thing . . . her unresolved issue was that of blood. What's yours? If you're not sure, pray David's prayer in Psalm 139:23 (KJV), "Search me oh God, and know my heart, try me and know my thoughts."

BRENDA L. CALDWELL., PH. D.

Deal With It or Die With It!

You may not realize you're dealing with an unresolved issue until God reveals it to you through prayer, speaking through someone, or by some other means. I once had a health issue that I avoided addressing for a long time. It started as a tiny knot, but since I felt fine, I never bothered going to the doctor. Over time it began to grow. I became afraid to go to the doctor, fearing that it was cancer. Eventually it grew to the size of a large egg, and Satan had me convinced that I had stage four cancer because I was beginning to experience episodes of throwing up along with severe stomach pain. Following each episode, I started to feel fine again, so I continued to avoid going to the doctor. One night, the pain became so severe that I could no longer avoid this issue. After seeing the doctor, I was referred to a surgeon who, without x-raying me, recommended immediate surgery to repair an inguinal hernia that occurred through strenuous exercise. Even though I was glad to know it was not cancer, I did not want to have surgery. I told the surgeon that as a woman of faith, I would just pray for healing and change my eating habits. The surgeon informed me that he was a man of faith, and that the hernia was not going to go away. I continued to delay the surgery for weeks, until suddenly, I felt led to ask for confirmation. Within one week, God sent a friend, a church member, and my grandmother to all say the same thing . . . "you should have this surgery." Finally, I consented only to find out that God used it to save my life!

Life Saving Truth

The surgeon did not discover until he opened me up that I had a rare hernia called a femoral hernia that had already become obstructed. If any bowel entered into my system and caused gangrene, this poisonous substance would have been fatal. Unknowingly, I was walking around, feeling fine, but with a potentially deadly hernia on the inside of me. God, who is the all seeing and all knowing, "Surgeon of surgeons," knew what my surgeon did not know. Had I not faced my fears and consented to have this surgery . . . death was eminent! What started as a tiny knot became a potentially deadly situation, all because I was not willing to face my unresolved issue. Without a shadow of a doubt, God's loving and merciful hand intervened. As the author of Lamentations 3:23 (KJV) proclaims, "His mercy is new every morning; how great is thy faithfulness." As you read this book, allow God to speak to your spirit. Receive the truth that you may not *want* to hear, but *need* to hear. It will save your life in a way that brings healing to your soul as we journey together toward "Mercy Hospital."

Take it from me. Avoiding or delaying any

unresolved issue will only make it worse. Therefore, face your "Uns" with the comfort of knowing that through Christ, you are more than a conqueror (Romans 8:37). It will only strengthen you to become a testimony for someone else. Like the woman with the issue of blood, my issue was in my body. Since you're reading *Surgery for the Soul: Healing for the Hurting Heart*, it is likely your issue is in your soul . . . your emotional heart. Don't be afraid to face your true feelings about something that may have occurred in your life that is yet to be resolved. As we go along, let God prick your heart to deal with any issues that you may have tried to bury years ago. As I said earlier, whatever is buried on the inside of you does not die. It will contaminate you. Therefore, it must be dealt with in order for your soul to experience true freedom.

Unresolved Issues Can Show Up at Unlikely Times

I remember sitting, years ago, at the funeral of my father who did not raise me. As I sat there, anger began to rise up in me. I thought of all the years that went by without having him in my life. As kind words were spoken about my father (by a brother who I met only the night before), I found myself steaming. Anger and resentment welled up in my heart. Until that moment, I never knew that I carried these feelings from childhood into my adult life. It took a few more years before I finally accepted the truth that I needed to deal with this nagging issue in my heart toward my father. It was the only way to be at peace. My issue was that of feeling rejected and abandoned.

As I said, we all have experienced some emotional issue that may stem from childhood or some other point in our past. However, an unresolved issue can cause a lifetime of pain that never heals because it's never been dealt with. One of the major unresolved issues that plagues hurting people has to do with pain experienced from parents. These issues include rejection, abandonment, neglect, lack of nurturing, lack of love, or some form of abuse. The emotional wounds of a parent can not only last a lifetime, but can also affect every area of life. We will examine this in more detail. Other fragmented relationships that can also lead to unresolved issues include a spouse or significant other, family members, children, friends, and even relationships at work or church. Remember, what makes an issue "unresolved" is that there has not been closure with the other person involved. Without closure, it can leave you with feelings of betrayal, sadness, regret, anger, resentment, retaliation, or bitterness, to name a few.

Taking Down Strongholds

Unresolved issues set you up to struggle with various strongholds that can take a lifetime to overcome. Basically, a stronghold means believing a lie to protect yourself. Some examples of strongholds include suspicion, doubt, bad attitude, control, hatred, manipulation, self-indulgence, fear, anger, denial, hostility, and of course, unforgiveness. A stronghold is what you rely on to defend and protect your right to believe something. In other words, a stronghold will cause you to justify your actions or beliefs. For example, you may believe you have a right to harbor unforgiveness even though the bible is filled with scriptures commanding us to forgive others as God has forgiven us. The problem with a stronghold is that it hurts you in the end because it can destroy your relationships, your peace of mind, your ability to give or receive love . . . and even your life! However, the Bible declares in 2 Corinthians 10:4-5 (NIV),

> "The weapons we fight with are not the weapons of the world. On the contrary, they have divine power to demolish strongholds. We demolish arguments and every pretension that sets itself up against the knowledge of God, and we take captive every thought to make it obedient to Christ."

This scripture means we have spiritual weapons like God's word that give us power to take control over every thought and make it pleasing to God. Proverbs 23:7 (KJV) declares, "For as a man thinketh in his heart, so is he." The truth is that it takes *humility* to acknowledge and confront a stronghold, whether it means admitting to hostility or hatefulness. This is the first step to overcome a negative thought pattern that keeps you in mental bondage. Admitting a stronghold means realizing that this pattern of thinking is harmful and no longer acceptable to you. Confronting a stronghold means making a decision to face and bring closure to the unresolved issues that created the stronghold in your mind.

When Emotional Needs are Not Met

The next type of "Un" that must be faced is *unmet needs*. These are feelings of emotional deprivation or lack of love, affirmation, and validation. The need to feel loved, affirmed, and validated is universal. It's true, studies show that childhood emotional neglect can be harmful later in life. Expressions of love and engaging touch is a foundation that should start in early infancy. Children who have not had ample positive physical, emotional, and verbal attention face higher risk for behavioral, emotional, and social problems as they grow up.

Many of the issues we see in our society today stem from unmet needs in childhood. These include teen pregnancy, addictions, drug use, high rate of abortions, pornography, illicit sexual behavior, domestic violence, and the escalating divorce rate. The human need for love, affirmation, and validation has led many people to make destructive choices that cause a lifetime of pain and regret. Most often, the first source of emotional neglect happens with parents because we naturally expect that our parents will love, accept, and nurture us in an environment that will help us develop into thriving adults. When this does not happen, it can lead to *arrested development*, which means being emotionally stunted at an age of trauma or neglect that occurred in childhood or adolescence. Another way to describe it is emotional immaturity.

Help, I'm Stuck!

It is highly possible to physically "grow up" and remain stuck emotionally at age ten if something emotionally traumatic happened at this age. For example, if, instead of being loved on, you were beaten on or often heard harsh "put downs" . . . you could still be emotionally filtering everything that happens to you through the eyes of an abused ten year-old rather than an emotionally stable adult. Say your mother or father physically, mentally, or verbally abused you. What if they rejected, abandoned, or neglected you? If so, then arrested development can play out every day in some way. Some adults who are capable of working a job, paying bills, and handling household responsibilities can act out like a child if they don't get their way. Some could have a hard time expressing true feelings or be emotionally detached from their spouse, children, or others.

Paul declares in 1 Corinthians 13:11 (ESV), "When I was a child, I spoke like a child. I thought like a child, I reasoned like a child. When I became a man, I set aside childish ways." With arrested development, however, it causes you to emotionally act the age you were when you "shut down." It shows up when acting out in a relationship with a spouse, family members, boss at work, friends, and so on. Every problem has a root. God created us to experience love in such a way that would so validate us, there would never be a need to "act out" to receive it. Yet, because of the soul-wounds suffered during childhood, many are still searching for dad's or mom's love. In a healthy soul, we see an ability to love unconditionally, understand deeply, and act and react appropriately and consistently with God's word. Healing past hurts or emotional wounds helps a person move toward that maturity.

Importance of the Family Blessing

Years ago there was a powerful book written entitled "The Blessing," by Gary Smalley and John Trent, Ph.D. The Family Blessing is a biblical act that began in Genesis 27:24-29. It is ordained of God and has been a Jewish custom since biblical times. The book emphasizes the blessing of a father to his sons. The patriarchs Abraham, Isaac, and Jacob all gave formal blessings to their children—and, in Jacob's case, to some grandchildren. Receiving a blessing from one's father was a high honor, and losing a blessing was equivalent to a curse.

The Family Blessing provides a sense of personal acceptance and protection and frees people to develop healthy intimate relationships. To bless is to provide a child with genuine acceptance and affirmation. It is also critically important for anyone who desires to draw close to another in an intimate relationship, because it establishes a bond of closeness. Blessing a child also releases him or her to become supernaturally empowered to prosper in every area of life (spiritually, mentally, emotionally, financially, and socially).

Five Steps to Release the Blessing

You see, from the beginning, it has been God's will that fathers would declare a generational blessing over their children. Spoken blessings can bring hope, encouragement, and direction for their lives. A child being affirmed and validated by parents has always been important to God because of the lasting impact it will have in shaping his or her life.

In "The Blessing," the authors share the five basic elements of the Family Blessing Ceremony:

1. Meaningful Touch

2. A Spoken Message

3. Attaching "High Value"

4. Picturing a Special Future

5. An Active Commitment to Fulfill the Blessing

*Meaningful Touch: This denotes drawing close to someone. It can be demonstrated in a kiss on the forehead or the hand, a hug or a gentle touch of the face. The absence of meaningful touch sets a child up for seeking it in unhealthy ways. Longing for meaningful touch can lead to harmful relationships and dangerous behaviors.

*A Spoken Message: A child needs to hear a spoken blessing from their parents. This can be words that express love and acceptance. Examples include: *"I love you. I believe in you. I accept you. I cherish you. I thank God for blessing me with you. You are a gift to me."* Proverbs 18:21 declares, "Life and death are in the power of the tongue." These are all powerful statements of affirmation that speak life and will definitely have a positive effect in guiding the course of a child's life.

There is something supernatural that happens when spoken words are released. Throughout the

Scriptures, we find a keen recognition of the power and importance of spoken words. In the beginning, God "spoke" and the world came into being (Gen. 1:3 KJV). In fact, nine times in Genesis chapter one, three powerful words are stated . . . "and God said!" Everything that he spoke came into existence! When he sent us his Son to communicate his love and complete his plan of salvation, it was his Word that "became flesh and dwelt among us" (John 1:14 KJV). God has always communicated his blessing through spoken words. He has given us power to do the same thing!

Spoken words of blessing should continue throughout childhood and adulthood as they affirm a child with love and acceptance. Spoken words of blessing also apply to marriage, friendships, and other important relationships. Absence of spoken words can lead to feeling a need to over-achieve or gain approval by succeeding at something. At the same time, it can lead to apathy, depression, and withdrawal. The reason many people hesitate to bless their children is simply because their parents never gave it to them. I believe it is only from lack of knowledge that parents would not release a blessing upon their child.

***Attaching High Value**: This means expressing to a child how much he or she is valued and cherished without words. It can be illustrated with bowing on bended knee, raising of arms, or an extended hug.

*Picturing a Special Future: Communicating a special future to a child is an important part of giving the blessing because it can greatly affect the person's attitude toward life. Children need to have a special future pictured for him or her. It means speaking forth a special future. These words help shape, mold, and guide them into the full potential God has for them. For example, *"God has a special plan for your life according to Jeremiah 29:11. God has plans to prosper you, not to harm you, plans to give you hope and a future. I see God's favor coming to you. I see you becoming all that God created you to do and to be. I see you prospering in life."*

*An Active Commitment to Fulfill the Blessing: This means expressing a verbal commitment to be in his or her life and see the predictions come to pass. It is a commitment to give unconditional love and acceptance, to pray for, to support, and to help guide. For example, *"I commit you to the Lord as I commit to pray for you, support you, listen to you, guide you, and help you become the person God created you to be. May the Lord watch over you and bless you all the days of your life. I bless you to live a life that honors the Lord."*

How wonderful the world would be if all parents participated in this powerful biblical principle of releasing the blessing upon their children. We would not have nearly the issues that daily plague our society. This is why so many people today are struggling with "father" issues. The absence a father's love and his words of affirmation are unmet needs that have left many adults "acting out" as a cry for acceptance and approval.

The same holds true for those who have yet to feel loved, affirmed, and validated by a mother who, for various reasons, is unable to meet this need.

Seven Affects of NOT Receiving the Blessing

Receiving a parent's blessing is so critical that without it, there are seven potential issues that people are susceptible to:

1. **Seekers:** Seeking love and acceptance in all the wrong ways; easily taken advantage of.

2. **Shattered**: Fragmented in their souls, emotionally wounded, and unable to connect to others.

3. **Smothering**: Needy, attention seeking, and easily taken advantage of.

4. **Angry:** Carrying anger rooted in rejection that affects relationships with others.

5. **Detached:** Emotionally shut down or withdrawn; unwilling to emotionally connect with others.

6. **Seduced:** Easily taken advantage of and drawn into

unhealthy behaviors.

7. **Driven:** "Over achiever;" having a strong need to achieve or gain approval in order to feel accepted, loved, or affirmed.

Even though this list gives succinct definitions of issues related to not receiving the Family Blessing, I believe it also cuts to the heart of why there is so much hurt, pain, and emotional suffering that wounded souls endure daily. As I mentioned, although relationships with parents are often the first root of emotional pain, it is also caused by other unresolved situations or circumstances. In any case, by now, you've likely identified with some of the "Uns" that have been revealed. Remember, we're on a journey to help you heal from any issues that need to be let go so you can receive your *new heart*.

Confession is Good for the Soul

As your empowerment coach and "spiritual surgeon," let me remind you, *God cannot heal until you get real.* So, at this point, on our journey toward "Mercy Hospital," as part of the pre-op, I encourage you to stop reading for a moment and take time to write a list of any "Uns" . . . unhealed hurt, unresolved issues, or unmet needs that you desire to be free from.

Remember, the more transparent you're willing to be, the more free you WILL be!

In chapter two, I will share how the effects of unhealed hurt, unresolved issues, and unmet needs lead to another major "Un" . . . the Unloving Spirit.

SURGERY FOR THE SOUL

BRENDA L. CALDWELL., PH. D.

2

WHO CRACKED YOUR MIRROR?

During a counseling session, a client once said to me, "I don't like what I see when I look at me." When I asked why, she replied, "There's nothing good in me . . . I think I'm worthless." So I asked, "Who told you that you're worthless?" She responded, "My mother told me she should have aborted me when she had the chance . . . so I think I'm worthless."

Years ago, someone coined the phrase, "Sticks and stones may break my bones, but words will never hurt me." I believe the person who first said this was either in a major state of denial or greatly deceived. The truth is that sticks and stones can break your bones, but *words* can break your spirit! My client's spirit was completely broken by the power of her mother's words. They destroyed her self-esteem, self-image, and self-worth! She hated looking at herself because her eyes could only see through the "cracked mirror" of rejection, abandonment, and self-hatred. Seeing ourselves through the eyes of a "cracked mirror" means having a distorted view of self. These cracks are caused by the cruelty of harsh words or other mistreatment inflicted by others.

So, who cracked *your* mirror? Or maybe the question should be, *what* cracked your mirror? Remember when I shared in chapter one that Satan is the biggest crack addict on earth? He looks for any cracks in your soul that he can use against you. The devil loves it when you have a distorted view of yourself. He knows he can torment you the rest of your life with issues like self-hate, self-doubt, self-rejection, self-loathing, and self-pity. This is what happens when you have not dealt with the "Uns" in your life.

The Unloving Spirit

Do you often have inner battles with a loudmouth voice constantly telling you you're not good enough, not worthy, not loved, not attractive, not accepted, or not valued? If so, let me reveal the truth to you . . . this voice has a name called the "Unloving Spirit." Ephesians 6:10 reminds us that we do not have a battle with people, but rather, our battle is with spirits. In his book, *Unloving*, Dr. Henry W. Wright describes the Unloving Spirit. It is a spirit that attaches itself to you to make you reject yourself because of something that was done to you or something you have done. It seeks to make you feel *unloved* and *unlovable*. It won't allow you to receive God's love. It won't allow you to love yourself.

It won't allow you to receive the love of others. Therefore, it prevents you from being able to express love.

It tells lies to make you feel guilty, ashamed, embarrassed, disgusting, unworthy, ugly, and unclean. It has a convincing voice! Like a skilled ventriloquist, the Unloving Spirit uses your lips to get you to curse your own life. It tells you things like, "Nobody loves you or accepts you the way you are." You then repeat what you hear, saying, "Nobody loves me or accepts me the way I am." It tells you, "You don't measure up because you're not smart like your brother and sister." Again, you repeat what you hear: "I don't measure up because I'm not smart like my brother and sister." On your way out the door headed to work, it can even make you late by telling you, "You need to change those clothes because you look fat in that outfit." Agreeing with the Unloving Spirit's voice can cause you to slip into a pit of self-inflicting pain for life.

Where Did God's Love Go?

The Unloving Spirit has three levels of separation. The first level is separation from *God*. It will torment you day and night with the thought that God doesn't love you because of what was done to you or what you have done. Whether you were mistreated in your past or did things you regret, the Unloving Spirit will not allow you to accept God's merciful gift of unconditional, unwavering love. This especially holds true if you have experienced issues in your relationship with your father like rejection, abandonment, neglect, or abuse. If you grew up unable to connect with your father because he was angry, judgmental, emotionally disconnected, or routinely critical, it can easily distort your view of God, perceiving him the same way. Take note, Romans 8:15 (NIV) refers to God as "Abba," which means, "Father God" or "Daddy God." It is God's will that we see him as our supremely loving Heavenly Father.

For this reason, fathers are charged with the responsibility to represent an image of God that demonstrates unconditional love for his children. He is a provider, protector, guide, and encourager. However, if you've struggled with having to earn your father's approval or acceptance, the real culprit is the *Unloving Spirit*. It wants you to believe the lie that God withdraws his love from you just like your father. The same holds true if rejection and abandonment came from the relationship with your mother. If you never felt the warmth of unconditional love flowing from her heart to yours, this can also distort your view of God. It may hinder you from experiencing a healthy relationship with him. By nature, mothers are designed to nurture their children with love. When this does not happen, it creates a breach in the soul that can take years to heal, or may never heal at all. In addition to parents, as we dig deeper, we will find the Unloving Spirit uses *any* relationship to destroy your ability to believe this statement: God loves you!

Bigger Bully Behind the Scenes

That's right . . . God loves you! In fact, he declares in Jeremiah 31:3 (NIV), "I have loved you with an everlasting love and with my loving kindness have I drawn you." From the beginning, God's love for us has been pure and untainted because he *is* love. God further cements his promise of unconditional love when he speaks through the Apostle Paul in Romans 8:38-39 (NIV), "For I am convinced that neither death nor life, neither angels nor demons, neither the present nor the future, nor any powers, neither height nor depth, nor anything else in all creation, will be able to separate us from the love of God that is in Christ Jesus our Lord." What a powerful promise from our Heavenly Father . . . NOTHING on this earth or in heaven can ever separate us from his love! However, why is it still a struggle for so many to accept this truth that is firmly planted in God's word? It's because of the ruling spirit behind the Unloving Spirit's mask called the "Anti-Christ" spirit. Allow me to explain what this spirit is in laymen's terms. First of all, "anti" means *against* or *opposes*. Anything that comes against written scripture is an Anti-Christ spirit because it seeks to convince us that the bible is not true. This is why in 1 John 4:1 (NIV), the writer declares, "Do not believe every spirit, but test the spirits to see if they are from God . . . " It is the Anti-Christ spirit that tells you Jeremiah 31:3 and Romans 8:38-39 do not apply to YOU!

Like a member of an organized mob acts real tough, but answers to a higher-ranking boss, so does the Unloving Spirit answer to the Anti-Christ spirit. The highest-ranking enemy behind it all is Satan who ultimately opposes us as God's greatest creation. So, it's important to understand there is a spiritual root to the struggle with accepting God's unconditional love. The Unloving Spirit receives orders to constantly bully you with the lie that God doesn't really love you. When you start agreeing with this lie, it starts to damage your faith, hope, and trust in God. Remember, the goal of Satan is to separate you from God in order to destroy your ability to have a healthy relationship with anyone else, including yourself!

Deep Truth, Deep Lie!

The deep *truth* is that God loves you. The deep *lie* is that he doesn't. This is why Paul declares,". . . that Christ may dwell in your hearts through faith. And I pray that you, being rooted and established in love, may have power, together with all the Lord's holy people, to grasp how wide and long and high and deep is the love of Christ, and to know this love that surpasses knowledge—that you may be filled to the measure of all the fullness of God" Ephesians 3:17-19 (NIV).

In this scripture, the Apostle Paul makes a case for why it is paramount we believe in how deeply God loves us through Christ. In believing so, we will forever be secure in to whom we belong at our core. A belief statement that summarizes this scripture is, *"My identity and my security is deeply rooted and grounded in God's love for me."* Being deeply rooted in God's love for you is like building a house on solid rock instead of quicksand! Come what may, a firm foundation in God's love has the power to sustain you through the storms and tornadoes of life.

This is precisely why the Unloving Spirit tries so hard to distract, discourage, and deceive you into thinking you are unworthy of God's love. It will whisper things like, "Your own daddy doesn't love you, so how can you expect God to love you?" "If God really loved you, then why didn't he protect you?" "Look at all the sins you've committed. You can never get right with God!" Of course, accepting these lies as truths will not only "crack your mirror," but will also affect your relationship with the Father. Feelings of shame, guilt, condemnation, and unworthiness all contribute to *cracking your mirror*. With the voice of the Unloving Spirit constantly in your ear reminding you of how unloved and unlovable you are, it is difficult to believe the promise in Psalm 139:14 (KJV) that you are "fearfully and wonderfully made."

Turning You On You

After the Unloving Spirit separates you from God, the second level is separation from *yourself*. Just as being separated from God can start early in life, so can separation from yourself. As I said earlier, this can start with degrading, spirit-breaking criticisms or put-downs that you grew accustomed to as a child and as you grew older. These include phrases like, "you're dumb," "you're so stupid," "you're worthless," "you're fat and ugly," "you're never gonna amount to anything," "you're gonna be just like your no-good father," "you're a mistake," "you can't do anything right," "you embarrass me," and the list goes on.

In chapter one, we discussed how God ordained spoken words to be released by parents to *bless* their children and shape their lives. To *bless* means to empower one to prosper in life. However, the above phrases represent the complete opposite. These cruel words have the power to curse a child's life. To *curse* means to empower one to fail in life. No child is born with high self-esteem or low self-esteem. As children, we are shaped by an environment that either nurtures us or neglects us. Words of encouragement, praise, and affirmation breed self-confidence, security, and sense of worth in a child's spirit. Words that criticize are belittling and demeaning. They breed the seed of low self-esteem, low self-worth, and self-rejection into a child's spirit.

Years ago I had a client who, at age 13, heard the most heart-ripping words from her mother that a tender teen could ever hear: "*I don't want you! I don't love you! Nobody else is ever gonna love you, not even God!*" Hearing these soul piercing words shoot out of the mouth of the very person who was charged with nurturing her, gave birth to unbearable pain that followed my client into adulthood. For years, she was emotionally stuck at 13 years old, unable to unlock herself from the prison cell of *arrested development.* She recalled how this emotionally fateful encounter with her mother caused her to immediately start reciting self-loathing comments in the mirror like, "I hate you," "You should've never been born," and "Nobody loves you, not even God!" Unfortunately, feeling stripped of identity and worth, she did what others who have been bullied by the Unloving Spirit do . . . *turned on herself!* For many of her adult years, she struggled with addiction, low self-esteem, self-hate, depression, and even sickness! Then finally, after years of running from her childhood pain, my client decided to face her "Uns." In doing so, her mind was transformed and she received a "new heart" that set her soul free! She is now healed mentally, emotionally, spiritually, and physically!

Disdain, Disgust, Detest

The scheme of the Unloving Spirit is to make you destroy your life by agreeing with abusive behavior or mistreatment inflicted upon you. Whether verbal, mental, emotional, sexual, spiritual, or physical abuse, you begin to blame yourself as if you deserved it. It also convinces you to turn on yourself when you have done things of which you are ashamed or regret. As I shared in chapter one, unresolved issues you have not healed from leave *cracks in your soul,* which in turn, *crack your mirror!*

With these cracks, the Unloving Spirit conditions you to carry out the following self-rejecting behavior patterns: You become your worst critic! You learn to put yourself down before anyone else can! You have a hard time accepting compliments! You struggle with giving eye contact in face-to-face conversations! You tell yourself that people don't like you! You compare yourself to others and feel less than them! You think others see your flaws when they look at you! You easily find fault with your appearance! You overly apologize for the smallest mistakes you make. At some point, like my client, you probably thought or said, *"When I look in the mirror, I don't like what I see."*

Rather than *loving* yourself, you tend to *loathe* yourself! To loathe means to hate, to have strong feelings of disgust, or to detest. This is exactly how the

Unloving Spirit wants you to feel, even for things you cannot control. With this wrong pattern of thinking, you're never at peace with yourself, day or night! In fact, some days you plain can't stand yourself! However, the fact remains, you can never get away from *you* . . . at least not physically. Thus, the separation that occurs within yourself is most often mental, spiritual, and emotional.

Was there something in your life years ago that still has you struggling with feelings of disdain, disgust, or detest toward yourself? This self-animosity can be the result of a wide range of childhood and adult issues such as bullying, rape, molestation, rejection, abandonment, physical abuse, verbal abuse, relationship breakups, addictions, choosing unhealthy relationships, and other bad life choices.

When Self-Pity & Pain Collide!

The Unloving Spirit also leads you to struggle with a spirit of Self-Pity. This means having pity for yourself concerning your difficulties or hardships in life. Self-Pity causes you to focus inward and keeps you stuck in your past. It programs you to say things like, "No one really cares about me," "No one understands what I'm going through," and "No one will listen to me."

With a self-pitying spirit, you may experience massive psychogenic pain which comes from the root word, psycho, meaning *soul*. It is physical pain caused by increased or prolonged mental, emotional, or behavioral factors. Psychogenic pain has no organic reason, nor is there really a problem . . . but there *is* pain, usually in the spine or muscles. Headaches, back pain, or stomach pain are some of the most common types of psychogenic pain. An example of this is fibromyalgia, a chronic condition of muscle and joint pain accompanied by fatigue. Self-Pity is a killer when it comes to producing psychogenic pain. In fact, when the Self-Pity spirit and physical pain collide, you may end up with an unnecessary hospital bill unless you choose to face your "Uns!" As I shared before, any unresolved or prolonged issues will only get worse. Remember, every problem has a root.

Self-Pity loves it when you compare yourself to others. They can be siblings, childhood friends, coworkers, family members, church members, social media "friends," or anyone else. It attempts to convince you that you don't measure up! When others seem to be doing well in life, the Self-Pity spirit steals your peace by getting you to ask, "What's wrong with *me*?"

"Packa" Lies!

The Unloving Spirit uses the back-up spirits of Self-Pity, Self-Rejection, and Self-Hatred to keep you in the bondage that something is wrong with you. These spirits also penetrate your soul, causing you to hold on to wrong words and demand that you conform to them. The writer of Proverbs 18:21 (ESV) declares that, "Death and life are in the power of the tongue, and those who love it will eat its fruits." Words have the power to build up or tear down, to heal or kill, and to lift your spirit or break your spirit.

Satan, the Father of lies, is banking on the hope that you will agree with lies spoken *about* you, *to* you, and *over* you! He knows that when you believe these lies, they separate you from you!

The question is . . . whose report are you going to believe? Will you believe the report of your mother, father, spouse, ex, family member, church leader, or someone else who cursed you with their mouth? Or, are you going to believe what God says about you? Paul proclaims, "Let God be true and every man a liar" (Romans 3:4, NIV). In other words, if what someone said about you is not in the bible, it's a LIE! The problem arises when you believe the lies.

Allow me to share an analogy about the danger of believing lies. Printed on the packaging of cigarettes is a warning that cigarette smoke can cause cancer. How? Smoking damages the cells that line the lungs. When a person inhales cigarette smoke, which is full of cancer-causing substances, changes in the lung tissue begin immediately. In the same way, when you started inhaling lies, they immediately began to damage the lining of your soul. Imagine for a moment a fictitious brand of cigarettes called "Packa Lies!" Each cigarette represents a lie. Each lie contaminates your thoughts and emotions with cancerous self-pity, self-rejection, and self-hatred, to name a few. Inhaling one lie after the next all day long is equivalent to being a "spiritual chain smoker!"

Inhaling Lies is Dangerous!

Inhaling lies from the Unloving Spirit is extremely dangerous to your physical health as well. For example, did you know that lupus is a painful autoimmune disease that causes the body to attack healthy tissues instead of things like bacteria and viruses? According to another book by Dr. Henry W. Wright entitled, "A More Excellent Way: Spiritual Roots of Diseases & Pathways to Wholeness," the spiritual root (although not all causes of lupus are spiritual) of lupus is self-rejection and self-hate! In other words, if Satan can get you to turn on yourself *inwardly*, it will eventually show up *outwardly*.

I shared this insight with a client a few years ago. She received a diagnosis that she was at the onset of having a lupus. I knew she had major self-rejection and self-hate issues due to childhood bullying. I told her if she would do the work to reconnect with herself she would experience a breakthrough in her health. She committed to receiving her healing by uprooting and falling out of agreement with the lies that controlled her life since childhood. It took a while, but when she returned to her doctor, she was informed that she no longer had any trace of lupus in her body! To God be the Glory! I will be sharing later how you too can uproot and fall out of agreement with any lies of the Unloving Spirit that have affected *your* life!

At this point, I want you to stop and consciously think about what lies you have believed about yourself for a long time. As we journey together, empowering you to receive your *new heart*, take a moment to write down all the hurtful words and phrases that continue to bother you. You will need this for a later chapter when you will be absolutely empowered with the spiritual tools to break free from every lie that has cracked your mirror! Be honest with yourself.

_____
_____
_____
_____
_____
_____
_____
_____
_____

An Assault on Your Relationships

The third separation of the Unloving Spirit is separation from others. What starts in childhood will show up in adulthood. In other words, after years of conditioning you to have a bad relationship with *yourself*, the Unloving Spirit then seeks to damage your ability to have healthy relationships with *others*. It uses tactics like fear, insecurity, low self-esteem, distrust, rejection, jealousy, envy, competition, lack of nurturing, lack of love, and *failed* relationships, to keep you from experiencing the *wholesome* relationships God desires for you.

As I shared before, arrested development involves being emotionally stunted at an age when pain or trauma occurred. It includes issues mentioned here and many more that creep up without warning in attempt to dismantle your ability to healthily connect with others. Years ago a friend of mine lived in such fear of domestic violence that, on her honeymoon, she pulled out a knife to show her new husband what would happen if he physically abused her. The real culprit influencing her actions was the Unloving Spirit. It convinced her to distrust that anyone could love her enough to treat her with honor and respect. Realizing she behaved with the emotions of a terrified eleven year-old, my friend realized she desperately needed counseling to heal from the childhood trauma of seeing her mother physically abused.

Fear is like the Unloving Spirit's deceitful cousin who seems trustworthy but leads you to make choices you regret later. It is rooted in lies! You may have heard of this acronym for the word FEAR: "False Evidence Appearing Real." There is another one as well . . . "Forget Everything and Run!" Fear says things like, "Don't you remember how you got hurt last time you trusted a friend?" "Don't you remember your father said you would never make it in business?" "Don't you remember your ex said no one else will ever love you?" Whether it's fear of rejection, fear of failure, fear of hurt, or fear of people, both of these acronyms describe the untamed power fear has, unless you stand up to it! We are told in 1 John 4:18 (NIV), "There is no fear in love. But perfect love drives out fear because fear has to do with punishment." Remember, when your belief is deeply rooted and grounded in God's love, it gives you power to silence the lying voice of fear.

Self-consciousness is also connected to the Unloving Spirit. Self-consciousness is heightened self-awareness whereby you feel uncomfortable or embarrassed about yourself.

Rooted in the fear of rejection, this leads you to

compare yourself to others and struggle with feelings of *not being good enough*.

If we struggle with accepting God's love and with loving ourselves, how then can we give or receive love from others? If this is you, remember, it goes back to Satan's deception, using the Unloving Spirit to perpetuate the lie that you are *unloved* and *unlovable*. How we see ourselves can affect the way others see us. In chapter one, I shared a list of the seven effects of not receiving the family blessing. These issues will often show up in unhealthy relationships. Allow me to share a few examples.

Five Reasons for Staying in Unhealthy Relationships

Unhealthy relationships are ones in which there is some form of physical, verbal, mental, sexual, emotional, or spiritual abuse. Signs of an unhealthy relationship include issues like control, anger, manipulation, blaming, shaming, co-dependency, and neediness. There are five reasons the Unloving Spirit can lead you to become entangled in unhealthy relationships.

1. Feelings of unworthiness

When you don't know how much you're worth, and when you haven't found a way to accept, honor, love, and respect yourself as God's creation (unconsciously or not), you will let others treat you poorly. In fact, you will find yourself settling for relationships that only *tolerate* you rather than *celebrate* you. Why? It's because deep down inside, you believe that to be normal. You believe that's what you deserve and thus, will find yourself staying in unhealthy relationships. An example of this is being a "seeker," searching for love and acceptance in all the wrong ways, therefore being easily taken advantage of. This comes from not having felt loved and affirmed.

2. Misconceptions about love and relationships

Paul declares in 1 Corinthians 13:4-7 (NIV), "Love is patient, love is kind. It does not envy, it does not boast, it is not proud. It does not dishonor others, it is not self-seeking, it is not easily angered, it keeps no record of wrongs. Love does not delight in evil but rejoices with the truth. It always protects, always trusts, always hopes, always perseveres."

As powerful as this passage is, when your foundation for what love looks like has been skewed by past mistreatment, it is difficult to expect this love from others. You may even forget that love doesn't abuse, love doesn't hurt, love doesn't shame, love doesn't blame, love doesn't condemn, and love doesn't control. Therefore, you may find yourself staying in unhealthy relationships, settling for less than God's best. An example of this is the "shattered" soul who is fragmented emotionally and unable to connect to others.

3. Dependency upon the other person

Emotional dependency is when you are entangled in a relationship with someone who is allowed to control your feelings of happiness. It means you need the validation and affirmation of a person to fulfill you. It means giving your heart to someone who has the power to break it. This is unhealthy and most often, negatively impacts your self-esteem and feelings of self-worth. An example of this is one who "smothers," meaning they are needy, attention seeking, and easily taken advantage of. Unintentionally, you become dependent on others to feel loved and accepted.

4. No way out

There are times when we want to leave unhealthy relationships. We want to have peace of mind and live a happy and harmonious life . . . but because of how bad things look, and because the road ahead seems foggy, we feel trapped. We can't seem to find a way out. We can't seem to find the help, encouragement, strength, and courage we need. So, we give up. If this is you, know there are resources available to help if you sincerely want out of an unhealthy relationship.

5. Loss of hope

Toxin from unhealthy relationships poisons the heart, mind, and soul. In doing so, it can corrupt the core of your faith, belief, and hope that your life will ever get better. With this comes the danger of giving up on love, giving up on yourself, and giving up on life. With the agony of defeat looming over you, you may find yourself staying in a hopeless, unhealthy relationship.

Staying in unhealthy relationships is pure deception from Satan using the Unloving Spirit to convince you that you're not worthy of love. It goes back to my original question, *who cracked your mirror?* The Unloving Spirit uses every tactic to distort your view of yourself and cripple your ability to have a healthy relationship with God, yourself, and others. It wants you to hold fast to the belief that no one, including God, will ever love you for who you are. This stronghold will do nothing but keep you strangled in the rope of insecurity, fear, performance, competition, envy, jealousy, and much more. In case you're wondering, it is never God's will for us to stay locked behind the bars of unhealthy, toxic relationships. He knows that Satan will try to use issues from our past to keep us in darkness. Because of his love, God will reveal the light of truth to set us free!

As we continue to journey toward receiving the gift of your new *heart,* God also desires for you to receive new *eyes* to see how much he truly loves you. In turn, you'll be able to fully love yourself and others. In chapter three, we will examine how the stronghold of bitterness must be confronted to start the process of healing of your "Uns."

3

BROKEN, BRUISED, AND BITTER

Battling with the "Uns" . . . unhealed hurt, unresolved issues, unmet needs, and the Unloving Spirit is enough to leave a person feeling *broken, bruised,* and *bitter.* Let's start with what it means to be broken.

A broken spirit destroys self-esteem, takes away joy in life, takes away dreams, and emotionally beats one down until he or she has no hope that life will get better. Breaking someone's spirit is often done by physical, mental, emotional, or sexual abuse. As stated earlier, it often involves verbal abuse as well.

When a person's spirit is broken, they often feel they aren't deserving of joy, or they may have lost all hope or desire for it. It's a feeling of total emotional defeat. This happens in many situations and settings. As I shared, it often starts in childhood with mistreatment from a parent, teacher, someone in authority, or even by other children. A broken spirit can also occur when a person is a victim of a violent crime, such as a woman who is attacked and gang raped by a group of men. Having a spouse ask for divorce or being fired from a job can result in a broken spirit because that person may feel rejected and unwanted. If not healed, this brokenness will play out in adulthood with various emotional issues.

The world is full of people with broken hearts, broken spirits, and broken relationships. Having a broken spirit can leave a person in a state of depression, which may result in suicidal thoughts. In many cases, the person has been conditioned to believe they aren't worthy of happiness or even life. In the Bible we read about a "wounded spirit" or a "broken spirit." The meaning of these two terms is similar. Both indicate distress. One person may have a wounded spirit in response to the same situation that results in a broken spirit for another person.

Some Say Broken, Some Say Wounded

What one person refers to as a broken spirit, another person may refer to as a wounded spirit. The writer of Proverbs 18:14 (KJV) declares, "The spirit of a man will sustain his infirmity; but a wounded spirit who can bear?" The same Hebrew word is translated as *broken* in Proverbs 17:22 (NKJV) where we read, "...a broken spirit dries the bones." The Hebrew word literally means "stricken." In both verses the NIV says "a crushed spirit."

A *wounded spirit* is one that is hurting, but so much that the hurt has festered into wrong attitudes and responses. A person with a wounded spirit lives with an inner misery that loves company! This spirit reveals itself in the following ways:

1. *A negative mind-set.* Those with wounded spirits are preoccupied with past hurts. They view incidents in life in the worst light. They see the bad and ignore the good. Their minds are filled with woes, suspicion, and assumption of evil.

2. *Victim reasoning.* With a wounded spirit, people view themselves as sufferers. They can even turn kindness of others into additional grievances . . . added pain. They are pleased when others notice their misery, and hurt when they do not.

3. *Grievance mannerisms.* Out of wounded spirits come sighs, groans, and exclamations that draw attention to the hurt. There's body language such as shaking the head, throwing dark looks, facial misery, and slumped shoulders. A grievance mannerism is the outward expression of a bad attitude.

4. *Blame tactics.* People with wounded spirits hold

other people responsible for the misery in their lives. In truth, people may have done them wrong but those wrongs shouldn't justify blaming others. Wounded spirits are able to cough up old hurts no matter what the present subject. They tell stories to put others in the worst light.

What oozes out of a wounded (broken) spirit is the foul smell of pessimism, self-pity, blame, criticism, and yes . . . a bad attitude! Is it any wonder in Proverbs 18:14 we are told, *"A wounded spirit, who can bear?"*

Bad Apple Bruise!

Now let's examine a bruised spirit. Have you ever dropped an apple and bruised it? You may not notice the bruise immediately. However, if you wait a few days, a large dark spot shows up. If you wait longer, the whole apple becomes rotten. Furthermore, if you put a bruised apple into a basket of apples, before long, the bad apple causes the other apples in the basket to rot as well.

An emotional bruise is much like the bruise of the apple. It may not show up immediately, but it causes a dark spot in someone's personality when it shows up. One may think an emotional bruise will go away in time, but instead, it gets worse. It can affect the entire personality. Furthermore, if you have a bruised spirit, you will likely "infect" those who come into contact with you most often. Your children, spouse, friends, and loved ones will be affected. Like the common cold, germs from a bruised spirit are contagious! For example, angry parents who often argue, yell, curse, and demean each other in front of their children will influence them to take on the same behaviors. In other words, angry parents often produce angry children!

15 Symptoms of a Bruised Spirit

Emotional bruises are generally deep and carry with them bondage. It's like dragging a ball and chain around with you wherever you go. The following is a list of fifteen symptoms that reveal a bruised spirit:

1. You are very defensive.
2. You are an overachiever.
3. You experience anxiety or panic attacks.
4. You are extremely passive to avoid any confrontation.
5. You belittle yourself.
6. You constantly seeking the approval of others.
7. You have a terrible short-term memory.
8. You often withdraw from others.
9. You struggle with various addictions (drug, alcohol, nicotine, sexual, or work).
10. You are hard to get to know.
11. You have memory blocks.
12. You get angry and lose control.
13. You experience episodes of crying.
14. You have a problem with habitual lying.
15. You have periodic nightmares.

It's important to note that you don't have to experience all these symptoms to be emotionally bruised. You may only experience two or three. Furthermore, when a person is bruised, he or she puts up a wall of defenses such as a critical spirit, pride, stubbornness, withdrawal, bragging, coldness, aggression, self-condemnation, passiveness, denial, and obsessions.

Weed of the Bitter Seed!

The issues associated with being broken and bruised can be traced back to the untamed stronghold of bitterness! Have you ever bit into something bitter? If so, most likely you immediately spit it out to rid your mouth of the taste. Why is it that, in seconds, we will rid our *body* of the flavor of bitterness, but allow the feeling of bitterness to contaminate our *hearts* for a lifetime?

Scripture speaks to the root of bitterness in Hebrews 12:15 (KJV): "Looking diligently lest any man fail of the grace of God; lest any root of bitterness springing up trouble you, and thereby many be defiled." Thus, the poisonous weed of bitterness can defile your whole spirit, and seriously hurt and defile many others as well!

Every good gardener knows that you can't mow over weeds. You've got to rip weeds up by the roots. Otherwise, they will keep coming back and when they do, they're bound to bring more and more of their *weedy friends*. It's no accident that God uses the image of a weed to describe a particular sin that has a way of creeping into all of our hearts . . . bitterness! Bitterness is *holding onto or showing feelings of strong animosity*. It grows beneath the surface, down deep in the soil of our hearts. It starts with little roots like jealousy, resentment, or hurt feelings.

The author's warning in Hebrews is clear. A bitter root will one day sprout and when it does, "many will become defiled." In other words, if that bitter root keeps growing, there will be a harvest of pain for you and the people in your world. This is what makes it extremely dangerous! However, sinful human nature makes it easy for us to justify harboring hurt feelings or grudges against others when we feel they mistreat us. In fact, we can feel this way towards God! I'll share more about being angry with God later.

Bitterness is a highly infectious spiritual disease that poisons others quickly if left unchecked. Like the bruised bad apple, it can ruin the whole bunch! The Bible warns us in 1 Corinthians 5:6-7 (KJV), "Know ye not that a little leaven leaveneth the whole lump? Purge out therefore the old leaven, that ye may be a new lump!" Like a tiny pinch of yeast will spread throughout an entire "lump" of dough and cause the whole thing to rise, people who are permeated with bitterness are a real burden and will pull everybody's spirits down. A bitter person often dwells on the negative and loves to murmur and complain. Remember, *every problem has a root!*

Four Ways to Spot a Bitter Root

It's wise to ask ourselves often, *"Am I bitter?"* Here are four questions to help you spot a bitter root in your heart:

Am I replaying the tapes?

Do you find your thoughts constantly fixated on a person who hurt you? Do you have a hard time getting this person off your mind? Do you find yourself angry when you think of this person? Remember Proverbs 23:7 (NKJV), "For as a man thinks in his heart, so is he." Replaying these tapes is a red flag that the seed of bitterness has taken root in your heart.

Is my mouth out of control?

Paul says in Romans 3:14 (NIV), "Their mouth is full of curses and bitterness." There's a strong connection between the words that come out of our mouths and the bitterness that takes root in our hearts. Do you find yourself losing your temper often? Are you critical, snappy, rude, judgmental, or sarcastic? It's possible the sins you're committing with your mouth are an extension of the bitterness that you have allowed to grow in your heart. From Luke we know that, "The good man brings good things out of the good treasure of his heart, and the evil man brings evil things out of the evil treasure of his heart. For out of the overflow of the heart, the mouth speaks" Luke 6:45 (BSV). When bitterness takes root . . . it causes the *mouth* to expose the corrosion in the *heart*!

Am I sick?

According to an article by Dr. Rick Nauert, bitterness, if left unchecked, interferes with the body's hormonal and immune systems. Bitter people tend to have a higher blood pressure, higher heart rate, and are more likely to die of heart disease and other illnesses. He also found that people who are bitter have more arthritis than those who are at peace. Similarly, they've discovered those who have a lot of fear in their minds (worries, tension, phobias, etc.) have more mental trouble, stomach trouble, and heart trouble. In other words, your state of mind and heart can actually poison your body (Nauert, 2015).

Of course, the Apostle Paul didn't have access to this scientific data when he wrote much of the New Testament, but that did not keep him from connecting the dots between bitterness and our bodies. In Acts 8:23 (NIV) Paul describes the "gall of bitterness." It's a vile, bitter substance that can literally make us sick.

The Seven Levels of Bitterness

The stronghold of bitterness is reinforced by seven

spiritual roots (also called spiritual dimensions). Another way of saying this is . . . there are seven levels of bitterness! After reading all seven, determine what level (dimension) you're currently at on your journey toward "Mercy Hospital."

1. Unforgiveness

When the root of bitterness gets a foothold, the first thing that happens is a record of wrongs (mental records of the wrongs done to you). Having flashbacks of something done to you that you cannot let go of is also unforgiveness. After unforgiveness gets a foothold and creates a record of wrongs done to you, the next level is resentment.

2. Resentment

Resentment means having bitter indignation toward someone who wronged you. When you have feelings of resentment, you think about this person in *your mind,* but feel them in *your heart.* Resentment is a foothold that gives a place for Satan to control your thoughts and emotions.

3. Retaliation

After resentment gets a foothold, it's revealed in another level of bitterness called *retaliation*. After resentment starts to simmer, you find ways to get back at the person who caused you to hurt. Retaliation seeks revenge. It wants to make the person pay. It says, *"It's time to get even!"*

4. Anger

After retaliation has a foothold, then *anger* sets in. Anger is the response to feeling violated. It says, *"I have a right to be mad at you for what you did to me!"*

5. Hatred

After anger sets in, another dimension called *hatred* arrives. Hatred is a feeling of animosity or hostility. To hate is to detest, despise, or to loathe. Hatred says, *"Because I remember what you did to me, because I've been meditating on it and I resent it, I'm going to get even. I'm going to add fuel to this fire. You don't have a reason to exist anymore, especially in my presence."* Hatred says, *"There's not even room on this planet for you and I in the same place, at the same time"* or, *"You and I cannot stay in the same room together."*

6. Violence

After hatred, in comes another dimension called *violence*. Violence is a behavior involving physical force intended to hurt, damage, or kill someone. Violence says, *"Before I eliminate you, you're going to feel my pain. You're going to hear my voice. You're going to know my hatred. You're going to experience it!"*

7. Murder

Once violence erupts, the final dimension of bitterness is *murder*. This can be actual physical murder, self-murder (suicide), or murder with the tongue, which is character assassination or verbal abuse. When hatred, violence, and murder are in someone's life, they feel that they are justified and everybody else is going to pay the price.

If any one of these seven dimensions of bitterness exists, all of the preceding ones will be there. For example, if you have hatred for someone, you're automatically holding unforgiveness, resentment, retaliation, and anger. Each dimension is progressively worse than the one preceding it. This is the reason that bitterness must be uprooted at the first sign. We are to "Get rid of all bitterness, rage and anger, brawling and slander, along with every form of malice. Be kind and compassionate to one another, forgiving each other, just as in Christ God forgave you" (Ephesians 4:31-32, NIV).

911 . . . Help! I'm Hurting & About to Hurt!

A few years ago, a man who was experiencing

overwhelming physical and emotional distress contacted me. He physically felt like he was having a heart attack, repeatedly making the statement, "My heart feels like it's about to explode!" However, he also kept saying, "I just wanna hurt him like he hurt my daughter!" I knew he was at a level seven on the scale of bitterness. After listening to his heartfelt plea for help, I was prompted in my spirit to conduct an immediate counseling session! I rearranged my appointments and scheduled him to come in for what I call an emergency therapeutic "heart surgery." In one session, this same man who had been tormented for over a year with thoughts of murdering a man for hurting his daughter, was able to forgive at the core of his being. To this day, he often tells me how much his emergency "heart surgery" saved his life physically, mentally, and emotionally. I was only a vessel.

It was the power of God that moved in his heart that day, after he did his part! This same gift awaits you!

What Level Are You On?

Now that you've read the seven levels of bitterness, honestly examine your own heart to determine what level you are on right now. As your empowerment coach and "spiritual surgeon," let me remind you that *God cannot heal until you're willing to be real.* You can change relationships. You can change churches. You can change jobs. You can even change states. Until you rid your heart of bitterness and unforgiveness, you will contaminate others wherever you go. Therefore, take a pen and fill in the blank with what your current level is:

_____
_____
_____
_____

In chapter four, we will explore the effects of the unforgiving heart and why forgiving is so hard for many to do.

SURGERY FOR THE SOUL

BRENDA L. CALDWELL., PH. D.

4
THE UNFORGIVING HEART

Happy people don't hurt people. Healed people don't hurt people. Hurt people hurt people. When we look around the world now there is so much anger, rage, hatred, and hostility! It grieves me to think that on any given day, there is a news story of a murder, road rage assault, or domestic violence incident. Sadly, this has become our norm . . . but it doesn't have to be this way. No one is *born* angry. Not one is *born* hostile. No one is *born* full of hatred and rage. It goes back to the need to *face our "Uns!"*

So many people are walking around with unhealed hurt, unresolved issues, and unmet needs . . . it's almost *unreal*! However, it *is* real. It's also a reality that as a society, we're conditioned from childhood to hold true feelings inside with statements like, "Be strong!" "Stop crying!" "What happens in this house stays in this house!" "Boys don't cry!" "Be a man!" Therefore, men don't want to be seen as *weak* and women don't want to be seen as *too emotional*. I believe this cultural thinking has damaged many people's willingness to confront their past! Again, what's buried on the inside doesn't die . . . it contaminates!

The Biggest "Un" of All!

This contamination has caused many people to be infected with the biggest "Un" of all . . . *Unforgiveness!* As I shared, having flashbacks of something done to you that you cannot let go of is unforgiveness. With an unforgiving heart, you refuse to pardon, free, or release someone of an offense against you. It also means refusing to extend the same mercy to others that God extends to you!

Harboring unforgiveness can be the result of many painful experiences, including divorce, relationship breakup, adultery, murder of a loved one, rape, molestation, bullying, being fired from a job, betrayal of a friend, family member, or church leader, rejection or abandonment of a parent, and any form of abuse.

Remember, a stronghold is unknowingly believing a lie and defending your right to believe it. Unforgiveness is a major stronghold that deceives you into believing you have the right *not* to forgive someone who wronged you. It's also a sin of disobedience to the word of God and is rooted in the Anti-Christ spirit. In Colossians 3:12-13 (NIV) we are commanded, "Therefore, as God's chosen people, holy and dearly loved, clothe yourselves with compassion, kindness, humility, gentleness and patience. Bear with each other and forgive one another if any of you has a grievance against someone. Forgive as the Lord forgave you." Children of God, this scripture instructs us to exhibit his character by showing compassion, kindness, and willingness to forgive others. However, when you've been hurt deeply and allowed the strongholds of bitterness, anger, resentment, and hatred to fill your heart . . . Colossians 3:12-13 *goes out the window*! The Anti-

Christ spirit uses your pain as a prime opportunity to convince you to reject the truth of God's Word, thereby, rejecting God! It *hates* written scripture because the Anti-Christ spirit knows that "all scripture is given by the divine inspiration of God and is profitable for doctrine, reproof, correction, and instruction in righteousness" (2 Timothy 3:16). In other words, the Anti-Christ spirit knows the Word of God has absolute power to transform your life if you will obey his commandments!

Getting Angry at God!

In my counseling practice over the years, I have encountered many clients who became angry at God after experiencing a painful period in life. For some, it was because they felt abandoned by God when they needed him most. For others, it was because they felt God caused them to suffer their pain. No matter the reason, the real culprit behind this thinking is the Anti-Christ spirit. As it partners with the Unloving Spirit to convince us God doesn't love us, the Anti-Christ spirit constantly schemes to damage our relationship with God by making him the blame for our pain!

The Anti-Christ spirit plants questions in your mind like, "Where was God when you were beaten and molested?" The more you meditate on this, you'll find yourself angrily voicing, "Where was God when I was beaten and molested?" The Anti-Christ spirit is also good at making you mad at God for things like relationship failures. It will whisper in your ear, "Why did God let your marriage fail?" Like a ventriloquist, you then repeat, "God, why did you let my marriage fail?" "Why did you let me be fired from my job?" "Why did you let my mom die?" "Why did you not answer my prayer when I kept crying out to you?" Satan, who rules the Anti-Christ spirit, ultimately seeks to "kill, steal, and destroy" our relationship with God by any means necessary (John 10:10). He knows that getting us to question God in our anger opens the door to a spirit of rebellion and disobedience to his Word.

When Sin Creeps In

Rebellion and disobedience is sin that starts in the heart. *Sin* is any action or behavior that breaks our fellowship with God. As the enemy of our soul, Satan loves it when we turn our hearts away from God. It gives him free reign to operate. Before long, sins like pride, anger, resentment, jealousy, and envy creep into the heart, further disconnecting our fellowship. Ultimately, Satan's scheme is to cause us to lose our faith in God. He knows, "without faith it is impossible to please God" (Hebrews 11:6). Satan also knows it is hard to have *faith* in God if you're *angry* at him. This is why he sends the Anti-Christ spirit to torment you with thoughts that keep you angry at God for the pain in your heart. Satan wants you to stop praying, stop reading the bible, stop going to church, and most of all . . . stop BELIEVING in GOD!

I Can't Forgive Myself!

Sometimes the anger in your heart is directed toward yourself. Are you struggling with not being able to forgive yourself for something in your past? Are you dealing with shame, guilt, or condemnation? Are you disgusted with yourself over a sin or wrong doing you committed that still haunts you? Shame involves having negative feelings about yourself, inwardly *turning on you*. It is the painful feeling of humiliation or distress caused by consciousness of wrong or foolish behavior. Guilt takes place when you realize what you've done and feel bad about the sin even after repenting of it. While guilt is seeing what you've done, shame is seeing yourself as a *failure because* of what you've done. Guilt is looking at the *sin* . . . shame is looking at *yourself.* The trick of Satan is to get you to so greatly meditate on the guilt that you turn on yourself with shame. The cousin to guilt and shame is condemnation. Condemnation is the knowledge that you're guilty of a sin and deserve to be punished, yet you feel unworthy of forgiveness.

Why is this so? *Satan calls you by your sin*. In 1 Timothy 4:13, he is the "accuser of the brethren." However, *your Father*, God, *calls you by your name*. He says in Isaiah 43:1, "I have redeemed you; I have called you by name, you are mine." Even with this powerful promise, people struggle to "forgive themselves" for something in their past. If this is you, please receive this revelation . . . *YOU CAN'T FORGIVE YOURSELF*! There is not one scripture in the bible that requires you to forgive yourself. In fact, there's not one scripture that makes it *possible* for you to forgive yourself!

God's Truth Strikes down Satan's Lies

This stronghold thinking is, once again, rooted in the schemes of the Unloving spirit and the Anti-Christ spirit.

The Unloving spirit tells you that you're unworthy of forgiveness. It partners with the spirit of guilt, shame, and condemnation to torment you for the sins and wrong choices of your past. The Anti-Christ spirit *so* opposes the bible, it works overtime to rob you of the peace that comes from receiving God's truth. It tells you, *"You can't believe these scriptures because you'll never be forgiven for what you did!"*

Whose report are you willing to believe? David tells us in Psalm 103:12 (NIV), "as far as the east is from the west, so far he has removed our transgressions from us." God also shares with us through Isaiah 43:25 (NIV), "I, even I, am he who blots out your transgressions for my own sake, and remembers your sins no more."

If you're going to walk in freedom from guilt, shame, condemnation, and any other spirit that has held you in bondage to your past, you must allow *God's truth* to strike down *Satan's lies*! Over 2,000 years ago, the issue of forgiveness was settled when God sent his beloved Son Jesus to die on the cross for our sins. Paul declares in Romans 4:25 (NLT), "He was handed over to die because of our sins, and he was raised to life to make us right with God." That's why "there is therefore now no condemnation to them who are in Christ Jesus" (Romans 8:1, KJV). If you are in Christ Jesus, meaning "saved" or "born again," you will not receive the judgment you deserve for your sins.

In 1 John 1:9 (NIV), the writer encourages us with the truth that "if we confess our sins, he is faithful and just to forgive us our sins and to cleanse us from all unrighteousness." You see, it is never a matter of you forgiving *yourself*! It is a matter of you *receiving* the forgiveness that comes from confessing your sins! When you do this, the court of heaven keeps no record of wrongs where you're concerned!

My Heart Won't Let Me Forgive Others!

If you're unwilling to *receive* forgiveness, likely you struggle with forgiving others. Have you ever made comments such as, "I will never forgive them for what they did to me?" "I may forgive but I won't forget!" "I want justice!" Many people have a hard time forgiving those who have hurt, abused, betrayed, violated, or otherwise wounded them. It's natural to harbor unforgiveness as a defense mechanism whenever someone's actions have caused us pain. It's also natural to want people to pay for what they did to us. It's called vindication! The need for vindication keeps your stomach in knots, your heart pounding, and your head hurting whenever you think of the person to whom you're harboring unforgiveness.

Danger of Anger

This self- torture is rooted in *anger*, which is the response to feeling violated or wronged. It means having strong feelings of hostility due to unresolved conflict in the soul. ANGER is only one letter short of DANGER! It is dangerous because, if not dealt with, anger can lead to an "explosion" of rage, resentment, and unrighteous behavior! Anger is also a "cancer" that destroys your peace, joy, health, relationships, and witness as a Christian. This is why Ephesians 4:31-32 commands us to "let go of all bitterness, rage, brawling, and anger . . .

and instead, be kind, tenderhearted and forgiving as God has forgiven us."

The bible speaks much about the importance of not being ruled by anger. Three scriptures I find helpful in the NIV reveal why anger is dangerous! First, Ecclesiastes 7:9 "Do not be quickly provoked in your spirit, for anger resides in the lap of fools." Reacting in anger will cause you to act in a way that is foolish and regretful. Anger will take you out of your character quicker than anything! Second, Ephesians 4:26-27, "In your anger do not sin; do not let the sun go down while you are still angry, and do not give the devil a foothold." This passage warns you to not let a day end in anger. Whatever you're angry about will only intensify. In doing so, this unresolved anger opens the door for Satan to have free reign to operate in your life. Third, the writer of Proverbs 22:24 warns, "Do not make friends with a hot-tempered person; do not associate with one easily angered." When people find out that you're easily angered, it will damage your reputation. It may cause others to not want to associate or be friends with you for fear of being hurt themselves.

The Unforgiving heart is one that harbors unresolved anger. Anger is another hidden tactic of the Anti-Christ spirit which tells you to ignore the warnings in God's Word. It says, "You have a *right* to be angry . . . look what they did to you!" "You *have* to act this way, otherwise people will walk all over you!" "They hurt you, so you need to get even!" The last statement is what gives an excuse for revenge. Revenge is the act of retaliating by inflicting pain or hurt on someone you believe has inflicted pain or hurt on you. Anger is hidden unforgiveness.

Endless Blocks

A stronghold of unforgiveness can block all mercy and grace from you because of an unforgiving heart. Peace and family harmony can be blocked. Prayers can be blocked. God's favor upon your life can be blocked. Divine healing can be blocked from your body, soul, and spirit. Unforgiveness blocks every area of your life!

Four Consequences of an Unforgiving Heart

1. Affects Your Prayer Life

It is definitely God's desire that you have a consistent prayer life filled with requests and a thankful heart knowing that your prayers will be answered. However, the *condition* of your prayers being answered is based on the *condition* of your heart. In Mark 11:25 (NIV) he says, "...when you stand praying, if you hold anything against anyone, forgive them, so that your Father in heaven may forgive you your sins."

Harboring unforgiveness has a major effect on your prayer life! It's important to God that you have a daily *heart check-up* to rid your heart of any unforgiveness toward anyone. Have you ever wondered why your prayers have not been answered? It could be because of your unforgiving heart.

2. Affects Your Health

Unforgiveness is the single most popular poison that Satan uses to attempt to destroy your health mentally, physically, emotionally, and spiritually. It is one of the deadliest spiritual poisons a person can take. Unforgiveness is like drinking a teaspoon of poison every day, and believing that the person toward whom you're harboring unforgiveness is going to die. Instead, the person slowly dying is *you*! Again, feelings such as anger and bitterness can cause everything from mental depression to health problems such as cancer or arthritis.

"Bitterness is a nasty solvent that erodes every good thing," says Dr. Charles Raison, associate professor of psychiatry at Emory University School of Medicine and CNN Health's Mental Health Expert. Feeling persistently resentful toward other people, like the boss who fired you, or the spouse who cheated on you, can indeed affect your physical health (Cohen 2011).

In fact, the negative power of feeling bitter is so strong that the authors of "Embitterment: Societal, Psychological, and Clinical Perspectives" call for the creation of a new diagnosis called PTED, or post-traumatic embitterment disorder, to describe people who can't forgive others' transgressions against them (Linden & Maercker, 2011). However, I don't believe bitterness is a *disorder*, but rather the result of *disobedience* . . . to the word of God!

As I shared earlier, bitter, angry people have higher blood pressure and heart rate and are more likely to die of heart disease and other illnesses. This is because feeling bitter interferes with the body's hormonal and immune systems, stated by Carsten

Wrosch, an associate professor of psychology at Concordia University in Montreal, in her chapter of "Embitterment" (Wrosch & Renaud, 2011).

Of course not everyone who has cancer or arthritis is walking in unforgiveness. However, constant bitterness and unforgiveness results in the faltering of bodily functions which opens the door to disease. According to Dr. Steven Standiford, chief of surgery at the Cancer Treatment Centers of America, refusing to forgive makes people sick and keeps them that way. With that in mind, forgiveness therapy is now being used to help treat diseases, such as cancer. "It's important to treat emotional wounds or disorders because they really can hinder someone's reactions to the treatments, even someone's willingness to pursue treatment," Standiford explained in a CBN News article. The article also sites research by Dr. Michael Barry, who states, "of all cancer patients, 61 percent have forgiveness issues, and of those, more than half are severe." Dr. Barry is a pastor and the author of the book, "The Forgiveness Project" (Johnson, 2015).

The conclusion of the matter is that there is a correlation between emotional health and physical health. The bible concluded this over 2,000 years ago. The writer of 3 John 2 (NIV) declares, "Beloved, I wish above all things that you will prosper as your soul prospers." Good health begins with letting go of an *angry, bitter, and unforgiving heart*!

3. Affects Your Relationships

Every one of us has been hurt deeply by someone else. As I shared, it may have been a parent, ex-spouse, current mate, sibling, former friend, relative, church member, boss, or perhaps a stranger. It could be a hurt that came from some violent or foolish act. It may be something that person *should* have done, but didn't. It may be something that was said to you. It could have taken place over many years, or happened in a moment. Regardless of who or what has your heart in a state of unforgiveness, it is detrimental to go through life unwilling to heal hurt and pain. The grip of unforgiveness, bitterness, anger, and resentment will damage your ability to *give love* and *receive love* in future relationships.

4. Affects Your Witness

Prayer is important. Praising God is important. Worshipping God is important. Using your spiritual gifts is important. Good deeds are important. However, according to 1 Corinthians 13:1-4 (NIV) there is something greater:

> "If I speak in the tongues of men or of angels, but do not have love, I am only a resounding gong or a clanging cymbal. If I have the gift of prophecy and can fathom all mysteries and all knowledge, and if I have a faith that can move mountains, but do not have love, I am nothing. If I give all I possess to the poor and give over my body to hardship that I may boast, but do not have love, I gain nothing."

It doesn't matter how spiritually gifted you are or how many good deeds you do, an unloving, unforgiving heart blows your witness as a Christian! If you're unwilling to forgive, *it makes your love walk weak.* In John 13:35 (NIV) Jesus confirms, "By this everyone will know that you are my disciples, if you love one another."

Hard Pill to Swallow

If only we would obey God's commandments . . . easier said than done. Even the disciples had questions. In Matthew 18:21-22 (NLT) Peter came to Jesus and asked, "'Lord, how often should I forgive someone who sins against me? Seven times?" "No, not seven times," Jesus replied, "but seventy times seven!'" In the context of forgiveness, I believe the hardest math problem in the universe is "What is seventy times seven?" It can be a hard pill to swallow. I don't know if Peter was hoping to hear a limit on the number of times we should be required to extend forgiveness to others, but Jesus made it clear . . . there is no limit!

In Matthew 18:23-35, Jesus shared a parable of a servant who received forgiveness of his debt. The unforgiving servant refused to extend the same mercy to a servant who was indebted to him. The unforgiving servant sent his fellow servant to prison where he could not repay the debt. In this parable, the unforgiving servant was sent to the torturers by the king (God) for his unwillingness to forgive others. We are often like this servant. We don't let another person off the hook. However, when we do that, we put ourselves in the place of God.

BRENDA L. CALDWELL., PH. D.

Wounders Need to be Forgiven

The bible promises that not only does God show mercy to *us*, but we *can* and *must* show mercy to each other. Grudges, getting even, and harboring unforgiveness are normal for the world scene, but they have no place in the life of someone enjoying the mercy of God. The bible also promises to bless those who mirror God's mercy: "Blessed are the merciful, for they shall obtain mercy" (Matthew 5:7, NKJV). It promises something else for those who refuse: "There will be no mercy for you if you have not been merciful to others" (James 2:13, NLT).

No matter how justified we *feel,* it will never be justifiable in the eyes of God to withhold the same mercy from others that we need from him. Think about it for a moment. Those who have caused hurtful wounds have to live with it for the rest of their lives. For many, the feelings of shame, guilt, and condemnation serve as daily punishment, but God gets no glory in this. Only *Satan* does. *Wounders* need to be forgiven because "all have sinned and fall short of the glory of God" (Romans 3:23, NIV). We've all sinned, caused hurt, or done something to wound someone else in life. We're all glad God is a forgiving God when *we* need his mercy. The same holds true for the *wounder* who wounded you! God loves this person just as he loves you. Jesus died for the sins of your wounder just as he died for your sins.

With a spirit of humility, meditate on the following questions: What if your wounder has been praying for forgiveness? Should God not answer their prayer just because you're the person who was wounded? What if your wounder has repented with a sincere heart? What if your wounder hasn't repented? What if the only way your wounder would know God is real is by receiving forgiveness from you? What if *you* were the wounder? Would you want to be forgiven?

What to do if the Wounder is You?

If you're reading this book and you *are* the wounder, receive this truth. If you're carrying a *burden* because someone refuses to forgive you, you have sinned against God! How? Because needing *someone else's* forgiveness more than *God's* forgiveness means you've made this person an idol in your life. No matter what, making *anyone* an idol is a sin. If you've hurt, wounded, or wronged someone, your responsibility is to admit it with remorse and ask forgiveness from those you wounded as well as from God. He will forgive you even if they *don't*. He will judge their hearts if they refuse to forgive you. Only do your part. Humbly reach out and ask for forgiveness. Make no *excuses*, but rather, seek to make *amends.* It takes humility to admit wrong and ask for forgiveness, but it frees your soul in the process. If you've already asked for forgiveness, then simply repent to God for making this person an idol and let him know that you receive his forgiveness and his peace into your heart. Allow God to do the rest. He knows *how* and *when* to prick the hearts of those you've wounded. Meanwhile, receive his peace and choose to let go of shame, guilt, and condemnation. It's also important for you to respect the fact that some people who forgive you will not always desire to continue a relationship with you. Accepting this will help you and the wounded person to heal and move forward.

You may be both the *wounder* AND the *wounded*. Either way, only the mercy gift of *forgiveness* can set your soul free! According to John 8:36 (KJV), "...he who the Son sets free is free indeed."

It's Time to Take the Cuffs Off!

Have you ever had handcuffs placed on you? Even if not, you can imagine how handcuffs make a person feel bound and controlled. Now imagine for a moment these same handcuffs being placed on your emotional heart. I call these *"heartcuffs."* When you are controlled by an unforgiving heart, you put yourself in a prison of pain. Shutting down your heart because of past hurts and unresolved issues is never healthy. It sets you up for strongholds of distrust, fear, suspicion, and many more. Just because someone hurt you in the past does not mean everyone else is going to hurt you. Staying angry over past hurts is a cheap trick of Satan. The risk of any relationship is that sometimes people *will* hurt us. However, putting on angry *heartcuffs* won't keep out *past pain*, it will only keep *future love* from entering in. Satan wants to make your past your future. God wants you to stop having an *affair* with your past so you won't *cheat* on your future!

It's time to take the cuffs off! It's time to let your heart be *revealed* so God can *heal*. If you desire to heal from an unforgiving heart, there's one powerful pill that works and has no negative side effects . . . *forgiveness*! As your empowerment coach and spiritual heart surgeon, I would like you to take a moment to list those issues that may be causing you to have an unforgiving heart. In chapter five, you will not only learn what forgiveness is, but will experience pre-op as we journey toward "Mercy Hospital" for the therapeutic *surgery for your soul.*

BRENDA L. CALDWELL., PH. D.

5
CHOOSE TO FORGIVE, CHOOSE TO LIVE

Do you know what the word *magnanimous* means? Years ago, I was standing next to a lady in church whom I overheard exhorting God . . . *"Oh God, you're such a magnanimous God!"* This description sounded so good I started saying it too . . . *"Oh God, you're such a magnanimous God. Hallelujah!"* I assumed it meant *incredibly big, huge, or amazing*! Without bothering to research its true meaning, in my daily worship time I continued to voice out loud, *"Lord God, I worship you because you are so magnanimous. I love you!"* Several months later, I was preparing to do a workshop on forgiveness. I was led in my spirit to look up the meaning of magnanimous. Would you believe this long word simply means *generous to forgive?* This is why God is described as magnanimous. He is generous to forgive *anyone* for *anything*. No matter what! Unlike God, many people are generous to *give* BUT too stingy to *forgive*. Many times, the same people who generously give away money, food, and clothing are the same ones who are unwilling to offer forgiveness to those who hurt them.

Five Reasons Forgiveness Can Be Hard

Why is forgiveness so hard? Denial, anger, bitterness, resentment, pride, fear, and rebellion all contribute to why many refuse to extend forgiveness. There are five wrong beliefs that also contribute to why it can be hard to forgive:

1. "I don't have unforgiveness issues."

Those who believe they don't have any unforgiveness in most situations don't truly know their own heart. In Jeremiah 17:9-10 we find, "The heart is more deceitful than all else and is desperately sick; who can understand it? I, the LORD, search the heart..." It is not wise to rely on your own wisdom. Rather, humbly ask God to reveal anything in your heart that is hindering your life. There may someone from your past who you've secretly held a grudge against, but suppressed it.

2. "I already forgave."

Have you ever found yourself having resentment, yet saying, "I already forgave them?" The truth is, saying the words *'I forgive'* doesn't mean anything if you don't have a change of heart. This is a trap! It's a deceitful tactic of Satan to keep you in denial of your true feelings. Look in the mirror and truly take an inventory before the Lord. Ask him if you already forgave to the fullest extent and with the purest heart. Do not be deceived in this area. It can steal your life! If you have any anger, resentment, bitterness, or feel separation from God, there's a good chance that unforgiveness is lingering. It's best to seek the Lord to ensure your victory and not allow yourself to live less than the abundant life he desires for you.

3. "If you only knew what they did to me."

The belief that what others have done is a reason to withhold forgiveness is one that causes many people to fall. What other people *did* do, *are* doing, or *will* do has no impact on the decisions that we are required to make in accordance with God's Word. Holding a grudge doesn't make you strong. It makes you weak. Forgiveness doesn't make you weak. It makes you strong. Allowing the sins of others to be the controlling factor in whether or not you choose to forgive is a set up for failure. It's willfully giving others control over your life. If you waste time focusing on what *they* did with a judgmental attitude, then won't you need forgiveness for that?

4. "It won't matter."

The lie that it won't matter if you forgive is a plot from Satan to keep you living in bondage. Anything that brings you closer to God is something that Satan does not want. Forgiveness is obedience to God which draws you closer to him. Satan will tempt you to believe that forgiveness does not matter; however, it *does* matter that you forgive. It's *your* life that is at stake. Believing a "Packa Lies" from Satan is dangerous to your well-being! He will send the Anti-Christ spirit to whisper, "You don't have to forgive them because they're gonna continue doing the same thing! You know they're not sorry for what they did, so it doesn't matter if you forgive them!" Entertaining these thoughts causes you to keep your *heart cuffs* on! You must understand that forgiveness matters because it sets *your* soul free! It matters because it shows you have a heart to obey God. It matters because there is no other way to experience renewed peace and joy. It matters because Jesus died on a cross for your sins and the sins of everyone who has ever sinned against you! When you refuse to forgive others, you deny your common ground as a sinner in need of forgiveness!

5. "They won't have to pay for what they did."

One of the biggest deceptions regarding an unwillingness to forgive is the thought, "They won't have to pay for what they did." This wrong thinking has ensnared many people into the bondage of self-inflicted hurt, pain, and mental suffering! Wanting others to pay for what they did is a *heart* issue. It means that your heart is consumed with anger, bitterness, and a need for *revenge.* Revenge means wanting someone to be inflicted with the same hurt or pain they caused you. In Proverbs 24:29 we are told, 'Do not say, "I'll do to them as they have done to me; I'll pay them back for what they did."' This is not the will of God, no matter how justified you feel in your thinking. In Isaiah 55: 8-9 (NIV) the Lord reveals, '"For my thoughts are not your thoughts, neither are your ways my ways," declares the Lord. "As the heavens are higher than the earth, so are my ways higher than your ways and my thoughts than your thoughts."' God's system is unlike the world's system. He requires us to obey his word and leave the rest to him. That's why in Romans 12:19 (NASB) we are warned, 'Never take your own revenge, beloved, but leave room for the wrath of God, for it is written, *"VENGEANCE IS MINE, I WILL REPAY,"* says the Lord' (emphasis added). We must allow God to administer justice in *his* way to those who have sinned without repentance.

Forgiveness is Not...

To understand what forgiveness *IS*, it's important to understand what forgiveness is *NOT!* The following is a list of what forgiveness is not:

1. Forgiveness is not tolerance.
2. Forgiveness is not pretending.
3. Forgiveness is not forgetting.
4. Forgiveness is not turning the other cheek.
5. Forgiveness is not looking the other way.
6. Forgiveness is not making a joke of a wrong done to you.
7. Forgiveness is not politeness or tactfulness.
8. Forgiveness is not a passive non-response.
9. Forgiveness is not a feeling.
10. Forgiveness is not temporary.

What is Forgiveness?

Forgiveness is a conscious act of the will to deliberately free, release, or pardon someone who has wronged you. Forgiveness is an act of obedience to God's Word. Forgiveness is an act of love. Forgiveness is the key to total healing, restoration, and freedom! It doesn't matter if your feelings have ceased, and it doesn't matter if God intends to judge the offender. God knows what the person(s) did to you, and he will bring good from it if you do your part, FORGIVE!

If You Don't, God Won't!

If you truly want to be set free, you must realize there are NO loopholes, like forgiving only when the other person admits they were wrong or asks for forgiveness. You are to forgive whether you have been asked or not. Forgiveness is so important to God that he made it an absolute mandate! In Matthew 6:14-15 (NIV) we are told, "If you forgive others, your heavenly Father will also forgive you. But, if you do not forgive others, neither will your heavenly Father forgive you." When you refuse to forgive, you cut yourself off from forgiveness. God will not forgive you until you obey his command to extend the same mercy to others that you desire to receive yourself. Mercy means *not* receiving the punishment we deserve. For a moment, think of the worst sin you've ever committed. Did you ask God for forgiveness? If so, he willingly extended mercy to you. As his children, God commands us to do the same! What happened in your past will not control the rest of your life once you make a conscious decision to forgive.

True forgiveness has a way of reducing a bad memory to nothing more than a fact from the past. It has no power to produce painful flashbacks or bad feelings. For example, when I was three years-old, I suffered a burn on my left hand and stomach while playing in the fireplace. I have a deformed finger as proof that I was burned. For years, I was ashamed of this finger until one day I realized it is symbol of survival! It doesn't hurt at all. I have no flashbacks! It's simply a reminder that I overcame a painful event in my life! When you're truly healed mentally, physically, or emotionally of a wound, you will no longer feel the pain associated with this memory.

When Surgery is the Only Option!

Many times, the problem with healing from pain is unwillingness to face the pain. As I shared earlier, my health issue that started as a tiny knot grew into a large hernia that became life threatening . . . all because I was unwilling to face the pain. The surgeon informed me that the only way to heal was to let him remove the hernia before it burst. If not, the hernia would eventually poison my bloodstream and kill me! Surgery was my only option!

In the same way, anyone who walks around with an unforgiving heart needs surgery in order to heal. Forgiveness is heart surgery that heals the soul! In the United States, heart surgeries are performed every day. According to the Texas Heart Institute, in a recent year, surgeons performed 500,000 coronary bypass procedures (2015). Even though there is a shortage of donor organs, according to Montefiore, more than 2,300 people undergo heart transplants each year (2016).

Heart problems can take you by surprise. Suddenly, you're hunched over with chest pressure, pain, or even a heart attack. These are frightening symptoms of coronary artery disease (hardening of the arteries). This disease means that your heart isn't getting enough blood. You may also be familiar with angina, one of the most common symptoms of coronary artery disease. Angina is a feeling that ranges from numbness or pressure to severe pain in your chest, arms, jaw, throat, or upper back. You might even confuse angina with heartburn. Sometimes you have no symptoms of coronary artery disease until you're struck by a heart attack. In any case, don't wait until chest pain or discomfort becomes severe before consulting a physician. The good news is that surgery and lifestyle changes give your heart another chance. Open heart surgery is any type of surgery where the chest is cut open and surgery is performed on the muscles, valves, or arteries of the heart.

If your *spiritual heart* is in trouble, God wants to perform an open heart surgery to heal your wounded soul. Unforgiveness, anger, resentment, bitterness, and hatred must be uprooted! If not removed, these emotional tumors will harden and eventually destroy every area of your life. FORGIVENESS is the only option! Period!

God knows every detail of why you feel the way you do. He knows what was done, what was said, what you've been thinking . . . everything! As the Surgeon of surgeons, if you allow him, he will give you a new heart. Why? Because God also knows you cannot forgive in your own strength. He says in Ezekiel 36:26-27 (NIV), "I will give you a new heart and put a new spirit in you; I will remove from you your heart of stone and give you a heart of flesh. And I will put my Spirit in you and move you to follow my decrees and be careful to keep my laws."

God is so loving and so amazing! Only he can open your wounded heart and take out the stony tumors that have weighed heavily on your soul! In doing so, he also empowers you to obey his word. In Psalm 119:11 (NIV) David declares, "I have hidden your word in my heart that I may not sin against you." Hiding pain, hurt, or anything that hinders your relationship with God is a sin. Meditating on God's word is the medicine that keeps you spiritually healthy.

Give Yourself Permission to Forgive

Pain, hurt, anger, bitterness, rejection, shame, guilt, abandonment, disappointment, regret . . . you can choose to do something about it. You can choose to *rehearse* your issues or *reverse* your issues. You can choose to be *victim minded* and oppressed or *victorious minded* and overcome. You can choose to stop walking in your *wounds* and start walking in your *worth*. Your past does not have to destroy or delay your destiny. Only you can give yourself permission to let go of past hurts. Only you can give yourself permission to forgive. When you choose to forgive, you choose to live!

Five Simple but Powerful Words

Let's look at the meaning of five powerful words that are critical to forgiveness:

1. Let: to give permission or to allow.

2. Go: to move away from.

3. Forget: to lose memory of.

4. Choose: to make a decision after considering all options.

5. Beguiled: to be tricked or deceived into doing something one thinks is right to do.

In the context of forgiveness, these five words make up the following empowerment statement: I have the power to let go of my past, forget the pain, choose to forgive, and never again be beguiled to walk in unforgiveness!

Steven's Story

I would like to share a story with you of how the above empowerment statement came to be. On February 24, 2000, my great-nephew Steven was born. God had already led me to dedicate him in the womb to be used in a special way. I felt an instant bond with him as if he was my own son. I knew in my heart Steven would be special. Little did I know just how special. When Steven was only one year old, he displayed an unusual love for God. He would joyfully sing praise and worship songs as well as clap his hands and pray in his own special way! It was amazing to watch him. He was also musically gifted. By age two, he was his own little "one man band," playing the guitar, drums, and keyboard. Some even called him "Lil' Stevie Wonder." Everyone loved Steven . . . our family, friends, church members, and everyone who came in contact with him. His bright smile lit up every room he entered. Steven's joyful spirit was absolutely contagious. By the time he was two and a half years old, he had such a zeal for God, he would preach and sing on his fireplace stage for hours.

Whenever he had an audience he would often tell us, "Say hallelujah, say praise the Lord, say thank you Jesus!" We all followed his leading, happily repeating whatever he told us to say. Steven was teaching us to have passion for God by being himself. It was obvious that God had a special plan for Steven's life. There was no doubt he was destined to become an anointed minister and a musician.

In One Moment

Suddenly, on July 24, 2003, at three and a half years old, Steven was brutally murdered! His precious life was cut short by the twenty one year-old boyfriend of Steven's mom at the time. Tragically, Steven was taken three thousand miles from home and beaten to death after enduring months of physical abuse. Nearly every bone in his body was broken, his skull was cracked, and bite marks covered his body. Hearing this devastating news felt like my heart was being ripped out with a piercing butcher's knife! To this day, I have never felt a pain like that day.

Six weeks before Steven was murdered, I was led in my spirit to go to a church I never attended before. I remember the pastor's words like it was yesterday, "Today's sermon is on forgiveness. How much are we to forgive? The answer: Anyone for anything, no matter what!" He then asked several scenarios such as, "What if someone raped you? What if someone abused you? What if someone murdered your child or a child you loved like your own? Again, we are to forgive anyone for anything, no matter what!" Three days after Steven's funeral, the Lord brought this pastor's sermon back to my memory, but I was not ready to forgive. I was too angry, hurt, grieved, and shocked. Ironically, I had just started my counseling practice. In theory, I knew I had to forgive. If not, it would have control over me.

At the time of Steven's death, his murderer showed no remorse at all. I was angry at him and I was also angry at God. I didn't understand why an innocent child who loved God so much wasn't protected from this vicious killer. My heart was heavy. I had no peace. I had no joy. A few weeks later I met a woman whose story changed my life. She told me that her dad and brother raped her for years but she forgave them. God revealed to her that her father and brother were both *beguiled*... deceived to think that their actions were ok. She realized in their "right minds," neither would have ever sexually violated her. Her decision to forgive them healed her heart. Hearing her story began to strip me of my defenses.

A few days later, I was convicted even more when I felt God speaking to my spirit this humbling message, "Daughter, I love Steven and I also love his murderer. My Son was murdered too!" At this point, I knew forgiveness was my only option if I wanted to be at peace.

On August 18, 2003, four weeks after Steven's death, I made the life changing decision to forgive his murderer. In a therapeutic manner using a chair, I said everything that I felt I needed to say. I expressed my anger and resentment! I told him how evil his actions were to kill this beautiful child! I expressed from the pit of my soul. *When I finished expressing my feelings, I acknowledged that he had been BEGUILED to think it was ok to take Steven's life. I remember saying, "As of today, I accept the truth that you were beguiled. In your right mind, you would never have murdered Steven." I then said the words that freed my soul, "Today, August 18, 2003, I CHOOSE to forgive you. I CHOOSE to release, to free, and to pardon you! You owe me nothing! You never have to say I'm sorry and you never have to ask for my forgiveness. I CHOOSE to forgive you just as God has forgiven me of my sins." I then asked God to forgive me of my sin of disobedience to his Word. I asked him to cleanse my heart of the anger, resentment, and unforgiveness. Next, I prayed a sincere prayer for Steven's murderer, asking God to forgive him and to heal his soul. I still wanted justice for his actions; however, it felt as if forty bricks had been lifted from my heart! Even though I still had to go through the normal grieving and healing process, my heart was made new that day! This one decision to forgive changed the course of my life!*

From Pain to Purpose

Little did I know tragedy would give birth to a ministry of forgiveness and healing that has now helped thousands of people around the world. Doors began to open for me to go places I never thought about to speak on the power of forgiveness. My absolute passion in life is helping others experience healing and deliverance from being wounded or abused. Whether it is one-on-one counseling or speaking at a conference, seeing people set free of past hurts blesses my soul beyond measure! God, in his sovereignty, did not stop Steven from being murdered, but certainly brought purpose out of my pain! His death gave birth to a ministry that has set many captives free from the bondage of unforgiveness, anger, resentment, bitterness, guilt, brokenness, abuse, and more. Though Steven's life on earth was only three and a half years, God revealed to me that he was an example of Jesus, whose ministry on earth was also three and a half years. *Steven* made every day of his short life count. Like Jesus, he was on assignment to "do his Father's business."

Still in prison at the time of this writing, Steven's murderer has never said "I'm sorry" or asked for forgiveness. The truth is I never needed him to say these things because I forgave him in my heart. I never again carried ill will toward him. Thirteen years later, while finishing chapter four of this book, I came across an anonymous quote, "I never knew how strong I was until I had to forgive someone who wasn't sorry, and accept an apology I never received." I felt led in my spirit to write a letter to Steven's murderer to let him know that he was forgiven thirteen years earlier. My sincere hope is that receiving a letter from me helped free his soul of any guilt, shame, or condemnation he may have been carrying for years. My choice to forgive him and to teach others to do the same has brought much honor to Steven's life and legacy.

In 2006, three years after his death, I received a special poetic tribute in memory of Steven in recognition of National Domestic Violence month. It was written by an attorney friend of mine who has worked for years to improve the lives of domestic violence victims.

Steven, Majestic Prince

God sent a child named Steven, into our midst,

Endowed with joy, hope and spiritual gifts.
And at the age of one, he was called to preach
Who would have thought a baby could be anointed to teach.
Then, his precious life was cut short and that
Seems to make no sense,
But, God had a higher plan for this majestic little prince.
He said, "First I'll use his life to bless everyone he meets,"
Then use his death to teach thousands about abuse, forgiveness and grief.
And here he is teaching God's people this very day,
Exposing Satan's plan to kill and steal our children away.
You were a warrior, Steven, and you are victorious,
Your time here on earth was blessed and glorious.
Your spirit even now graces us with power and might,
Encouraging us not to give up the fight!
'Til all of the captives are truly set free,
And all of the abused can dance and shout the victory!
So, little Majestic Prince, Steven, or Crowned Warrior,
Which is the meaning of your name,
Your life was full of meaning and your death was not in vain!

By Dorothy Ingram Miller, Esq.

I pray Steven's story has encouraged you to realize no matter how devastating or painful your wound is, you have the power to forgive and see good come out of it. In Romans 8:28, Paul declares, "And we know that for those who love God all things work together for good, for those who are called according to his purpose." In life, all things will not look good, feel good, or be good, but God has a sovereign way of bringing good out of every situation for those who love him and are called to fulfill a purpose! Sovereign means God can do or allow anything he chooses, even when we do not understand it. Our job as God's children is to trust him when we can't trace him, keep our faith when we can't figure him out, love him when we feel lost, and forgive those who *hurt* us so he can *heal* us.

In chapter six, we finally arrive at "Mercy Hospital" where you will undergo therapeutic heart surgery. As your spiritual surgeon and empowerment coach, I encourage you to open your heart to receive the new heart that awaits you.

6
THE SURGERY: A NEW HEART FOR A NEW START

Stop Looking in Their Piggy Bank

Imagine for a moment you need two hundred fifty dollars to pay a bill. You call someone who you think should have it, but the response you get is, "I only have two dollars and forty nine cents in my piggy bank right now. That's all I have to give you." Do you have a right to be mad at this person? NO! If all they have in their piggy bank is two dollars and forty one cents, you have no right to be mad. *Why? They cannot give you what they don't have.* This analogy is an example of why for many, it is hard to forgive. Expecting someone who hurt you or wronged you to give you what they don't have is like asking someone for a certain amount of money they just don't have.

If your father or mother never showed love for you, affirmed you, or gave you the nurturing you needed, it's highly likely they never received it from their parents. The truth is, no matter how you feel, you have no right to be angry at them. It's time to "stop looking in their piggy bank" because they do not have enough to give you what you need. Accepting this truth helped me to forgive my father for never being a part of my life. I realized that he couldn't give me what I needed because he was an alcoholic running from the pain in his own soul. When I finally confronted him therapeutically, even though he had already passed away, it brought so much healing to my soul. God changed my heart toward my father. I realized that his greatest gift to me was his seed that brought me into the world to do what I was born to do.

Only God is able to make up for what a parent or anyone else cannot give you. *Only his love, acceptance, and approval* can fulfill the innermost parts of your being. In Psalm 27:10 (NIV) we are encouraged, "Though my father and mother forsake me, the LORD will receive me." Therefore, to crave your parents love or anyone else's love more than God's love is a sin. It means you've made them an idol. The first commandment is "you shall have no other gods before me" (Exodus 20:3). There is NO human love that can compare to the love of God.

No Love Like Our God's Love

It's his desire that you receive this deep, unwavering love he has for you. In Ephesians 3:17-19 we are exhorted,

> "...so that Christ may dwell in your hearts through faith; and that you, being rooted and grounded in love, may be able to comprehend with all the saints what is the breadth and length and height and depth, and to know the love of Christ which surpasses knowledge,

that you may be filled up to all the
fullness of God."

Here's a powerful belief statement that summarizes Ephesians 3:17-19: *My identity and my security is deeply rooted and grounded in God's love for me.* Can you grasp how deep and how wide God's love for you is? His desire is that you would receive this revelation and allow his love to complete you. Don't let the way others have treated you affect how you feel about yourself! Let only God's thoughts define you! Being deeply rooted and grounded in God's love enables you to be secure in your identity as a person of worth. It is God's opinion of you that should matter and no one else's!

You cannot control if your father rejected, abandoned, or hurt you. His actions do not negate God's great love and acceptance of you. Simply accepting the fact that your father's seed helped give you life is freeing. If for no other reason, you can be thankful for this. His imperfections are okay because you have a heavenly Father who loves you perfectly. I shared with you that his name is Abba which means "Daddy God" or "Father God." When you choose to forgive your earthly father for what he couldn't give you, your Abba Father can fulfill your need for a dad's love beyond what you can imagine. Through forgiveness, God's desire is to give you a new heart so you can experience his love in a new way.

The same holds true if your mother rejected, abandoned, or hurt you. Her actions do not negate God's amazing love for you! She too may have missed the mark, unable to give you the love your heart desired from her. It's ok because God has the power to give you a mother's love. He is called El-Shaddai which means he is the Almighty many-breasted One who nourishes and supplies. His love can heal your heart like the loving touch of a nurturing mother! When you choose to forgive your mother for what she couldn't give you, you can receive a maternal love from God as El-Shaddai.

THEY LIED!

If those who wronged you have never made amends using words like, "I'm so sorry, I apologize, will you forgive me?" . . . there's a good reason. It's highly likely they don't know how. They have not allowed God to change their hearts. Stop looking in their piggy banks for what you need. You should never expect someone whose heart has not changed to make amends with you. Sometimes their shame, pride, guilt, or embarrassment stops them. If you're waiting for those who hurt you, abused you, or wronged you to apologize before you extend the gift of forgiveness, you will miss out on the abundant life Jesus died for you to receive.

Remember, Satan does not want you to forgive. He knows you will experience incredible freedom in your soul! His M.O. (mode of operation) is LIES! In fact, John refers to him as the "father of lies" (John 8:44). His lies may have caused you to feel unloved, unwanted, and unworthy! When you are tempted to believe him, remember what Paul says in Romans 3:4, "...let God be true and every man a liar." It only matters what God thinks, says, and feels about you! It doesn't matter what anyone else ever thought about you, said about you, or felt about you. THEY LIED! How do I know? If it can't be found in God's word, it's a LIE! The question is . . . are you willing to forgive those who lied to you?

The Power to CHOOSE!

If I can forgive a murderer, you can forgive anyone who caused pain in your life. You can forgive your father. You can forgive your mother. You can forgive your ex. You can forgive your abusers. You can forgive anyone for anything, no matter what. Whether it may be church hurts, childhood hurts, family hurts, friendship hurts, or other relationship hurts, you can forgive. How? You have the power to CHOOSE! This really is an empowering word! It means having the ability to make a decision after considering all options. Let's examine the options of whether or not to forgive. Option one: *hold unforgiveness*. With this option comes continuous anger, resentment, bitterness, strained relationships, health dangers, bad attitude, loss of friends, loss of respect, etc. Option two: *release forgiveness*. With this option comes supernatural healing in your soul, freedom to move forward, peace, joy, new and renewed relationships, mercy, spiritual growth, and the favor of God.

As I shared, forgiveness is not a feeling. You may never *feel* like forgiving someone who hurt you. Forgiveness is not tolerance. It doesn't mean you have to allow them to be a part of your life. If you need to forgive someone who is toxic, you can do so without remaining in an unhealthy relationship. You have a right to set boundaries and have healthy relationships that *enhance* your life rather than *hinder* your life.

BRENDA L. CALDWELL., PH. D.

Don't Ban Yourself from Friendships

It is definitely God's will for you to have healthy friendships that add value to your life. In Proverbs 17:17 it is written, "A friend loves at all times." True friends will be there for you through the ups and downs of life. According to Proverbs 18:24, ". . . there is a friend who sticks closer than a brother." Sometimes, however, friends may disappoint, betray, or hurt you. If you're harboring unforgiveness towards any past or present friends, the best decision you can make is to forgive them so you won't ruin future friendships. Don't let a few friends who disappointed, betrayed, or otherwise hurt you, destroy your ability to develop new friendships. Don't be beguiled by Satan to shut down and ban yourself from ever accepting friends into your life again. Satan wants you to take an experience from your past and make it your future. *God wants you to stop having an affair with your past so you won't cheat on your future!* We all risk being hurt when we open ourselves up to friendships or any other relationships. The writer of Proverbs 4:23 warns you to "*guard* your heart," not shut down completely.

Some years ago, in the middle of experiencing a difficult financial crisis, I felt rejected and abandoned by a close friend whom I thought would be there for me. Her attitude seemed judgmental towards me rather than compassionate. In fact, she disappeared from my life without any explanation when I thought I needed her friendship the most. It was hurtful and shocking, but for my own need for closure, I chose to forgive and release her! Within three months, God sent me two beautiful friends who I've come to cherish as sisters! God will do more than you can imagine if you will obey his Word. He will help you to trust and love again, if you will do your part. FORGIVE.

When Trust has been Crushed!

One of the major consequences of being betrayed or wronged in a relationship is the violation of trust. A violation of trust can take years to heal or cause further damage in the process. Satan's plot is to entangle us in a web of distrust so that future relationships will suffer as a result of the actions of someone from our past. Let's face it. At some point in life our trust will likely be crushed; however, we all have violated someone's trust, whether intentionally or unintentionally. This is why a willingness to extend mercy to others is so important. If you've put up a wall of distrust to protect yourself from ever being hurt again, you've only hurt yourself by missing out on the opportunity to develop new relationships that God desires to bring into your life. So, as you prepare for your "heart surgery," ask God to help you learn to trust again. The most powerful way to start is by choosing to trust him. The psalmist says, "It is better to put your trust in the Lord than your confidence in man" (Psalm 118:8, KJV). As humans, we will let each other down, but God can be trusted at all times. It's now time to trust him to heal your hurting heart!

Mercy Hospital

We've been on a journey and now we're here! We've arrived at a special place called "Mercy Hospital," where God wants to perform a supernatural heart surgery that will enable you to extend the gift of mercy to others and receive it back from him in return! This mercy gift is wrapped in a package of seven letters that have the power to remove emotional tumors from your heart and give you a merciful heart that is willing to forgive anyone for anything, no matter what. What are the seven letters? . . . F-O-R-G-I-V-E! This is the heart surgery that heals the soul.

The time has come for the surgical moment in your life you have needed! This is the moment to face your "Uns!" It's time to remove the cancer of unforgiveness caused by unhealed hurt, unresolved issues, and unmet needs in your soul. You've read the truth throughout this book. FORGIVENESS is the only option to experience true healing in your heart. Remember, this is for YOUR healing. The person(s) you need to forgive does not have to physically be in the room with you. This is what makes it therapeutic surgery. It is also therapeutic vindication that will empower you to express what you need to say without experiencing interruption, denial, or offense. If you open your heart and your mouth with sincerity, it will be as real as if the person is in the room. When you are ready to go through the "surgery" process, use the following as a guide after first praying for God's strength and presence to be with you.

Surgery for the Soul . . . Receive Your New Heart! Seven "How To" Surgical Steps to Forgive & Be Free

Please read the instructions before starting these steps. Before you begin, take a moment to prepare your mind and spirit so that this experience will be as authentic as it needs to be for you to experience your "surgery for the soul." If you know in your heart that you are ready to forgive and move forward, follow these seven steps of therapeutic heart surgery:

Step 1. In preparation for therapeutic surgery, you can first write a letter to help process your feelings. Writing a letter is optional as it could help you formulate your thoughts and feelings. It is not to be given to the person(s) you are confronting. It's a tool to help you recall the hurt and pain that may be buried deep in your soul.

The letter should address the person(s) by name to include the following example: "Dear   . I am writing this letter to confront you because I am ready to forgive you, but first I have some things I need to express. (This is when you can express all the feelings you have held inside). Conclude with: "Because I desire to be free, I CHOOSE to forgive you." Note: If you do not need to write a letter to help you process your feelings, start with Step 2.

Step 2. Find a space where you have privacy to express yourself verbally. Use two chairs, one to sit in and the other to face with the person's name written on a piece of paper. This will allow you to confront the person(s) as if he or she is in the room with you. NOTE: It is more effective to repeat these "surgical steps" for each person you need to confront. Also, if possible, play soft instrumental music in the background to help set the atmosphere. This is optional.

Step 3. Close your eyes to prepare your mind and spirit to verbally express what you have been holding inside. Meditate on what your feelings and thoughts are until you know you are ready to express them verbally. At this point, open your eyes, take a deep breath, and state the name written on the paper. Use the following as a guide. More than anything, speak from your heart. Begin with, (Name), "I am confronting you today (state date) because I am ready to forgive you and be set free. First I have some things I need to express. (This is when you will express all the feelings you have held in. Example: "I'm angry at you! I resent you! I hate you!" Then express why you have these feelings. Example: "You raped me! You rejected me! You abused me! You betrayed me!" Next, express how their actions hurt and affected you. During this critical time of purging your soul, you must be as transparent as you need to be. Remember, God cannot heal until you get real! Remember, his Spirit is with you every step of the way!

Step. 4. Once you have said everything you needed to say, you will be at another critical stage in therapeutic surgery. This is when you must humble yourself to realize that this person's actions were rooted in one word: BEGUILEMENT. You can use the following as a guide: "Now that I have said what I needed to say, I accept the truth. The only reason you (express what they did to you) is because you were BEGUILED! You were tricked and deceived into thinking it was ok for you to (repeat what they did). In your right mind you would never have (repeat what was done) me. I also accept the truth that I was BEGUILED to think that I had a right to harbor unforgiveness, anger, bitterness, hatred, resentment, etc. toward you. I have no right to harbor unforgiveness toward you and also expect God to forgive me of my sins. No matter how justified I felt, I was wrong. I have sinned because of my disobedience to God's Word. So, TODAY (state date) I CHOOSE to forgive you. I CHOOSE to release you, to free you, to pardon you! You owe me nothing! You never have to say "I'm sorry" and you never have to ask for my forgiveness. I CHOOSE to forgive you just as God has forgiven me of my sins."

Step 5. Pray from your heart a sincere prayer of repentance. Acknowledge your sin to God and ask him to forgive you according to 1 John 1:9 where we are told, "If you confess your sins he is faithful and just to forgive you and to cleanse you from all unrighteousness." Ask God to also cleanse your heart and heal your soul of the stones of unforgiveness, bitterness, resentment, anger, hatred etc.

Step 6. Pray a special prayer for the person you have forgiven. Ask God to help you pray a sincere prayer for this person as a way to seal the healing that took place in your heart. As Jesus said on the cross, "Father, forgive them for they know not what they do," ask God to forgive the person who hurt you. You will know the seed of forgiveness took root if you are willing to pray for this person's well-being. To help you with this step, ask God to give you a new, *magnanimous* heart. Pray the following: "Lord, I sincerely ask you to give me a magnanimous heart like yours, one that is generous to forgive anyone for anything, no matter what. By faith, I receive my new heart in Jesus name." Take a moment to thank God for giving you a new heart.

Step 7. Just as a physical heart surgery takes time to fully heal and requires rest and recuperation, when you finish, be sure to take time to rest your spirit, soul, and body! It is wise to sit quietly for a while as you would if you were sent to the recovery room after a physical heart surgery. You can use this time to listen to soothing music and have additional prayer time. Now, as a physical heart surgery requires daily medicine to strengthen a new heart, so does a spiritual heart surgery. To strengthen your new spiritual heart and reinforce your choice to forgive, start meditating daily on the medicine of God's word (Colossians 3:12-13, Ephesians 4:29-32, Psalm 119:165, and Matthew 6:14-15, for example). Getting God's word in you has the power to transform your soul and spirit. "For the word of God is alive and active. Sharper than any double-edged sword, it penetrates even to dividing soul and spirit, joints and marrow; it judges the thoughts, and attitudes of the heart" (Hebrews 4:12, NIV). The more you meditate on daily scriptures about forgiveness, the more your heart will become conditioned to quickly forgive anyone for anything, no matter what.

Step 1. In preparation for therapeutic surgery, you can first write a letter to help process your feelings.

Post-Surgery Notes

Note 1: Choosing to forgive does not mean you won't still have feelings for a while. Healing is a process. It will take time for your feelings to catch up with your decision to forgive. Also, depending on the extent of your emotional hurt, you may still need professional counseling to help you. This is healthy and advisable if you feel you need further assistance on your journey toward wholeness.

Note 2: If a person does not know you have been harboring unforgiveness, you do not have to tell that person you have forgiven them. A "therapeutic surgery" is for *your* well-being. However, if someone knows that you have being harboring unforgiveness toward them, the most powerful display of humility you could demonstrate is by first admitting you were wrong to harbor unforgiveness and then ask for their forgiveness. Along with this, your willingness to express your forgiveness will likely strip the person's defenses and give room for God to work on his or her heart. Remember, your willingness to free this person's soul will free your soul even more. This act of humility wins every time! Pray and be led by the Lord.

Note 3: If any feelings such as resentment or anger try to resurface, take authority over these feelings by consciously making the statement, *"I CHOOSE to forgive (person's name) just as God has forgiven me."* Making this declaration will strengthen you day by day until your heart is completely healed. Satan has no place in your soul when you release wrong feelings and choose to speak words of life!

As your empowerment coach and spiritual surgeon, I pray you use these surgical steps as a guide to help you receive the healing from hurt and pain your heart deserves and desires. I have used this guide many times since it first helped me to forgive Steven's murderer years ago. I have found it to be effective because I always invite the presence of God to be with me as I walk through the steps. It is inevitable that we will experience hurts that will require us to extend the mercy of forgiveness to others. Making it a lifestyle to forgive quickly will enable you to experience a deeper level of peace, joy, and freedom in your soul. Most of all, remember, when you choose to forgive, you choose to live!

In chapter seven, you will discover the favor that follows forgiveness!

Addendum: Response Letter from Steven's Murderer

In a fashion that could only have been orchestrated by God, shortly before this book went to publishing, I received a letter from Steven's murderer. Unbeknownst to me, he received my letter on his thirty-fourth birthday! He was sent to prison for second-degree murder and aggravated child abuse at age twenty-one.

As I began to read his letter, I was brought to tears by the remorseful way he expressed his sorrow for what he had done to Steven. I admit it was a very painful letter to read because he was brutally honest about his actions. Certain parts were almost unbearable. However, he shared with me that for thirteen years (at the time of this writing), he had been asking God for two things.

First, he was praying for forgiveness and a way to express his sorrow to my family. Second, he was asking God how he, someone with no history of mental illness, could hurt an innocent child to the point of death. Continuing to read, I noticed that he stated my first name over and over, calling me *Ms. Brenda*. He respectfully acknowledged me in a way that truly opened my heart to receive his apology as he poured out his heart.

If you recall, I shared in chapter five that when I wrote his letter, I wanted him to know he had already been forgiven for the past thirteen years. I also told him there was no need to ask for my forgiveness, nor did he have to respond to my letter. In his letter back to me, he did not ask forgiveness. He simply thanked me over and over for forgiving him. He said, *"Ms. Brenda, you truly have the heart of an angel because only God could have opened it up to me."* He asked me to continue praying for him and to write him again. He went on to say how good God is to answer his long time prayer to be forgiven! His sincerity reminded me why God desires for us to have *His* heart . . . the *magnanimous* heart!

Reading his letter brought my calling full circle. It confirmed all the forgiveness principles that God led me to teach over the years. For so long I've shared that the moment we forgive and release our offenders, God begins to work on their hearts as well. This is exactly what happened when I chose to forgive on August 18th, 2003, though it took thirteen years for it to be revealed to me. This letter also confirmed that God loves those who *wound* as much as He loves those who are *wounded*. He heard this man's prayer and answered it at the right time. For thirteen years, he was thought of as "Steven's murderer." Thirteen years later, he became "the young man who blindly took Steven's life." Only God could have orchestrated for him to receive my letter on his birthday. What a loving gift from a loving God! Remember how I shared in chapter four that *wounders* need to be forgiven? It's true. It really does give God room to work on their hearts and set their souls free!

Since then, I have written another letter to further free this young man's soul. I explained to him what it means to be *beguiled* as the true reason why he took Steven's life. Only God could have answered his prayers through a family member of the very child whose life he took. Out of respect for his privacy, I will not mention his name, though he has offered to do anything to honor Steven's memory. At his request, I will continue to pray for him and send letters as the Lord leads. I have faith that he will make Jesus his Lord and Savior. I can truly say that receiving his letter is a gift. It humbly inspires me to continue what God has called me to do . . . minister hope, healing, and deliverance to wounded souls, no matter who they are!

7
GOD'S FAVOR FOLLOWS FORGIVENESS

Making forgiveness a lifestyle is life-changing! A heart that forgives is a heart that lives. A heart that lets go of hurt is a heart free of pain. A heart that forgives is a heart that knows true joy and peace. A heart that forgives is a heart that reflects the love of Christ. A person who has a heart to obey this commandment will experience the flow of God's favor in every area of life!

"Favor" is blessings from God. You do not deserve these blessings nor can you explain how you received them other than by God's hand. Favor is displayed in many forms. It may include wealth, tangible gifts, connections, doors of opportunity, wisdom, compassion, faith, peace, knowledge, etc. We are told in second Chronicles 16:9 (NKJV), "For the eyes of the LORD run to and fro throughout the whole earth, to show himself strong on behalf of those whose heart is loyal to him." The scripture shows that not everyone has a heart committed to God's ways, therefore, he rewards those who are. God loves all his children, but those who are loyal to obey his commandments will find his favor following their lives. I believe the favor of God can do for us in one day what we could take years to accomplish alone. Isaiah declares in 1:19 (KJV), "He that is willing and obedient shall eat the good of the land." God desires to bless those whose hearts desire to obey his commandments. Obeying the commandment to forgive shows others that the love of God dwells in your heart.

No One Can Make You Mad!

As you desire to experience a continuous flow of God's favor, hold on to the following true statements: No one can MAKE you mad or angry! No one can MAKE you hate! No one can MAKE you resentful! No one can MAKE you bitter! No one can MAKE you feel hurt! We allow these cancerous tumors to invade our hearts based on how we respond to various offenses. Sadly, people will say and do awful things throughout your life that may hurt, wound, or offend. When this happens . . . you have power! You have power to CHOOSE how you will respond. You can CHOOSE to hold onto your anger, or you can CHOOSE to release your anger and forgive. You can CHOOSE hate, or you can CHOOSE to let go of hate and forgive. You can CHOOSE to harbor resentment, or you can CHOOSE to release resentment and forgive. You can CHOOSE to hold onto hurt, or you can CHOOSE to release the hurt and forgive!

Life happens. Hurt happens. Betrayal Happens. How we respond determines what comes next. This is called attitude. Attitude is our response to life's circumstances. We have the power to choose whether we will be controlled by a negative attitude or a positive attitude no matter what happens in life or in our relationships. Satan loves it when we respond in a negative manner. God loves it when we respond in a positive manner. The only way to respond to hurts, wounds, and offenses God's way is by becoming rooted and grounded in God's word. As I shared, Second Timothy 3:16 reminds us the bible ". . . is profitable for doctrine, reproof, correction and instruction in righteousness." The bible is here to help us learn to do the right thing even when it is difficult. The truth is, when you honor God, God will honor you! He shows us this truth in Luke 6:32-36 (NKJV):

> "But if you love those who love you, what credit is that to you? For even sinners love those who love them. And if you do good to those who do good to you, what credit is that to you? For even sinners do the same. And if you lend to those from whom you hope to receive back, what credit is that to you? For even sinners lend to sinners to receive as much back. But love your enemies, do good, and lend, hoping for nothing in return; and your reward will be great, and you will be sons of the Most High. For he is kind to the unthankful and evil. Therefore be merciful, just as your Father also is merciful."

The above passage is a powerful example of how God's ways are not our ways. As a society, we've become conditioned to treating others the way they treat us. This opens the door to revenge, anger, resentment, grudges, etc. Instead, God expects us to treat others the way he would treat them . . . with love.

BRENDA L. CALDWELL., PH. D.

The Matthew 5:44 Principle

If you desire to honor God and experience his favor, the "Matthew 5:44 Principle" will challenge you and change you for the good. In this verse, we are implored to "love your enemies, bless those who curse you, do good to those who hate you, and pray for those who despitefully use you and persecute you." Below, the verse is broken down to explain each principle:

1. **Love your enemies:** Biblical agape love is the highest form of love that serves regardless of circumstances. This weapon of love has absolutely no defense. In Ephesians 5:1-2 (NIV) we are told, "Therefore be imitators of God as dear children. And walk in love, as Christ also has loved us and given himself for us, an offering and a sacrifice to God for a sweet-smelling aroma." When you choose to walk in love with those who have wronged you in any way, you demonstrate that Christ is real in your life.

2. **Bless those who curse you:** In Ephesians 4:29 (NIV), Paul warns, "Do not let any unwholesome talk come out of your mouths, but only what is helpful for building others up according to their needs, that it may benefit those who listen." No matter how tempted you are to speak badly about those who have wounded or cursed you, choose to speak *well* of them instead. It will bless you beyond measure! In John 6:63, Jesus told the disciples, "...the words I speak, they are spirit and they are life." Imagine the peace you would have by making it a habit to do what Jesus did. Speak life!

3. **Do good to those who hate you:** As you go through life, you will likely experience being hated, disliked, or mistreated for various reasons. The natural reaction is to have the same response. However, doing the opposite brings glory to God and rewards for your life. In Proverbs 24:22 (NKJV) it is written, "If your enemy is hungry, give him bread to eat; And if he is thirsty, give him water to drink, For so you will heap coals of fire on his head, And the LORD will reward you." Your kindness toward those who've wronged you or mistreated you will wear them down like coal in a fire! It will cause them to wonder what makes you different.

4. **Pray for them that despitefully use you**: It goes totally against human nature to pray for those who have caused hurt or harm in your life. In fact, the only way you'll be able to do this is by remembering what it means to be beguiled. Knowing they were "deceived to think their actions were ok," you'll be empowered to pray for them with a pure heart. This is not an easy thing to do, but the more you practice praying for those who hurt you, the more peace you'll experience.

Don't Take the Bait!

"The Bait of Satan," by author John Bevere, is a book that gives excellent insight on how Satan works to get Christians caught in the trap of offense! There is a spirit of offense that is growing more and more prevalent in the world. It results in marriages ending due to "irreconcilable differences," friendships breaking down, and relationships being destroyed. It leads to church splits, petty lawsuits, domestic violence, and even murder. We can't be ignorant of Satan's tactics and fall for his tricks. I believe offense is Satan's number one weapon against Christians. Offense is annoyance or resentment caused by a perceived insult against or disregard for oneself or one's principles.

We have all been offended, and we know of others who have been hurt as well. However, offense is not some innocent little thing we can choose to hang onto until we feel like letting go of it. Offense is a serious issue, a weapon designed by Satan to rob you of God's best and to steal the future God has destined for your life. Offense causes a person to shut down to God's way of handling the problem and build a wall with a gate that only opens to those who agree with them.

The spirit of offense chokes ordinary conversation with people because you view every word they speak through the eyes of your hurt. It hinders your ability to give people the benefit of the doubt. It suffocates forgiveness and tolerance. It denies human imperfection. It judges. It criticizes. It assumes the worst.

When you've been offended by someone, do you not want to hear what the Bible says about forgiveness? No! Offense's job is to make you not want to listen to God's way of rectifying the situation. Furthermore, if you get offended and don't rectify the problem, a stronghold forms to protect your "right" to stay offended. Being held captive to this thinking will prevent you from receiving what God wants you to have.

The Favor of Peace

The cure for offense is found in Psalm 119:165 (KJV), "Great peace have they which love thy law and NOTHING shall offend them." The powerful revelation in this scripture is that meditating on God's Word can fill you with such peace, you won't be insulted or resentful about anything! Can you imagine living your life in such a way that NOTHING offends you? Wouldn't it be awesome if the words and actions that were intended to offend you "rolled off your back" like water? According to the psalm given above, it is possible to live an "offense-free life." God promises that if you love his Word enough to obey what it says, you'll have so much peace in your life that NOTHING will offend you! Peace is a premium gift to the soul. That's why Jesus says in John 14: 27 (NIV), "Peace I leave with you; my peace I give you. I do not give to you as the world gives." Meditating on God's Word will help you discern when Satan is trying to snatch your gift of peace away.

It's also important to keep in mind that we never have battles with people, but rather, with spirits! So when you feel offense trying to entrap you, remember that behind the scenes is a spirit of anger and beguilement in operation. Stop and ask yourself, "Why am I getting offended?" The Spirit of God will reveal the truth to help you release the offense before it takes root. This is why praying to receive a magnanimous heart is so powerful. Being quick to "forgive anyone for anything, no matter what" will change your life! It dissipates, dismantles, and dissolves Satan's plan to steal your favor, peace, joy, hope, health, and relationships.

The Favor of Debt Cancellation

Matthew 6:12 commands us to forgive our debtors as we are forgiven of our debts. In the Greek, the word debt literally means *financial obligation*. In the Aramaic, it means *sins*. In any case, we are commanded to forgive others of their debts against us so that we will be released of our debts.

A few years ago, I was harboring anger and resentment toward my former financial planner who wrongly advised me to make a decision putting me $21,000 in debt. To make matters worse, in the midst of this unresolved issue, he disappeared! I was crushed because I trusted his financial advice and thought highly of him. For months I received calls from a bill collector. I knew I had to do something, but didn't know what. I decided to pray a sincere prayer for God's intervention. What I heard next in my spirit was almost audible, "Repent for harboring unforgiveness in your heart and I will free you of this debt." Immediately I fell to my knees and repented for blaming my financial planner and harboring unforgiveness, anger, and resentment against him for a decision *I* chose to make. I took responsibility for my own actions. I humbled myself before God with a sincere heart and surrendered the debt completely to him that day. Then a miracle happened. I never heard from this company again! Unbeknownst to me, six months later I received a letter stating my debt was discharged! This experience taught me a great lesson about how God's favor follows forgiveness! I believe the golden nugget in Matthew 6:12 is that God wants to supernaturally release us from *our* debts as we humble ourselves to release *others*, whether from financial debts or sin debts.

The Favor of Answered Prayer

God takes delight in giving us the desires of our hearts. He loves to show himself mighty by answering our prayers in his way and in his timing. Meanwhile, we're commanded to walk in faith and forgiveness. Both are important in the sight of God in order to please him. In Hebrews 11:6 (KJV) we're told, "Without faith it is impossible to please God because anyone who comes to him must believe that he is and that he is a rewarder of them that diligently seek him." We must walk in faith to please God. He also commands that we walk in forgiveness. In Mark 11:25 he shares, "When you stand praying, if you hold anything against anyone, forgive them, so that your Father in heaven may forgive you your sins." Maintaining a forgiving spirit keeps God's ear open to your heart's desires and allows favor to follow your prayers! You must "therefore confess your sins to each other and pray for each other so that you may be healed. The prayer of a righteous person is powerful and effective" (James 5:16). Favor follows the prayers of those who live to honor God's commands.

The Favor of Blessed Relationship

God honors the relationships of those who have magnanimous hearts. They are generous to forgive anyone for anything, no matter what. This demonstration of Christ-like character does not go unnoticed by the Father. The seeds of a forgiving heart will produce a harvest of blessed relationships with your spouse, family, friends, coworkers, church members, business associates, and even strangers. According to Psalm 5:12, God will cause his favor to surround you like a shield. He will cause people to go out of their way to bless you. As you purpose to walk in agape love and rise above the pettiness of offense in your relationships, you will experience the favor of Luke 2:52 … "increase of favor with God and with man." In Psalm 90:17 David wrote, "Let the favor of the Lord our God be upon us and establish the work of our hands." As you choose to make forgiveness a lifestyle, God takes delight in lavishing you with his supernatural favor that is undeniable, unexplainable, and unstoppable!

Favor Declaration

A declaration means to speak over your life that which you desire to see come to pass. It's said in Job 22:28 (KJV) that, "You will also declare a thing, and it will be established for you; so light will shine on your ways." The following is a daily declaration that will empower you to walk in faith, forgiveness, and unmerited favor!

"I declare that I am walking in faith and forgiveness and therefore receive the favor of God in every area of my life. I declare that I have a magnanimous heart that is generous to forgive anyone for anything, no matter what! According to Psalm 90:17, the favor God is upon the work of my hands. In fact, the favor that follows me is undeniable, unexplainable, and unstoppable!"

As your empowerment coach and "spiritual surgeon," I highly encourage you to learn the above declaration by heart. Life and death are in the power of the tongue. Speaking this powerful declaration is a way to condition your mind and spirit to obey God's commands and receive a continuous flow of favor for your obedience!

In chapter eight, we will conclude our Surgery for the Soul journey together by empowering you to come into agreement with what God says about you as the final authority in your life!

BRENDA L. CALDWELL., PH. D.

8
I LOVE WHAT I SEE WHEN I LOOK AT ME

When I was six years old, I remember being able to spell "hippopotamus." More than forty years later I admit I need spell check. The point is, I thought I was a smart kid! That is, until I entered the first grade. On the first day of school, I recall running into the classroom with excitement in my little heart about the possibilities of learning new "big words." In less than twenty seconds, like a shot-down eagle, my spirit broke when I heard my teacher yell that deathly phrase, "SIT DOWN, DUMMY!" Her words pierced me like a knife. Something on the inside shut down at that moment. I was psychologically paralyzed. I never got past that traumatic first day. I was called "Dummy Caldwell" nearly every day of my first grade year. I knew for whatever reason, my teacher didn't like me, so I didn't like me. I felt worthless, intimidated, and ashamed every day. My teacher, charged with the responsibility of building me *up*, seemed to enjoy the twisted thrill of tearing me *down*. Consequently, I failed first grade and had to repeat it the following school year.

This time an amazing bond happened on the first day of school. My new first grade teacher knew I failed the previous year. I still remember her life changing words, "Brenda, you are so smart. You can learn anything you put your mind to, and I'm so glad you're in my class!" These words watered my soul. With each passing day, her words lifted my spirit and confidence like a high-flying kite. Under her loving care, my broken wings were mended.

Recognizing an artistic gift in me, she entered me in a citywide art contest in which I won first place! I received a plaque, a hundred dollar savings bond, and was featured on the local news. Today, in addition to my other work, I am a commissioned artist with paintings that hang on the walls of businesses and homes throughout the country and abroad. Why? Because my *second* first grade teacher was on assignment from God to heal my wounded spirit. She put my self-esteem and self-confidence back on the right track. Earning a doctorate in 2001, I often think about the impact of my beloved teacher. She would be so proud to know the same little girl, once called "Dummy Caldwell," is now respectfully called "Dr. Caldwell." Her impact on my life was so profound. Her name says it all. *Mrs. Pentecost!* The book of Acts tells about the day of Pentecost when believers were filled with the power of the Holy Spirit. Believe me, the day I met Mrs. Pentecost, I received the power to believe I was smart after all! I share this story to demonstrate how words and treatment have a profound effect on our *self-esteem, self-confidence,* and *self-worth!* My original teacher "cracked my mirror." My new teacher "mended my mirror."

Remember the question, "Who cracked your mirror?" It's time to empower you to *mend* your mirror! It doesn't matter who "cracked your mirror" to make you feel unloved, unwanted, or unworthy. The real culprit is the Unloving Spirit. According to Second Corinthians

10:5, "We demolish arguments and every pretension that sets itself up against the knowledge of God, and we take captive every thought to make it obedient to Christ." The Unloving Spirit allows those pretenses to take root . . . and it has been allowed to rule your thought life long enough! You have power to disagree with the lies from this tormenting spirit and agree with God's truth about you. Whose report are you going to believe? The report of your BEGUILED mother, father, spouse, ex, family member, teacher, church leader, or someone else who cursed you? Or, will you believe what God says about you? In Romans 3:4 (NIV) Paul declares, "Let God be true and every man a liar." If what someone said about you is not in the bible, it's a LIE! This includes the following phrases: "You're dumb." "You're so stupid." "You're worthless." "You're fat and ugly." "You're never gonna amount to anything." "You're gonna be just like your no-good father." "You're a mistake." "You can't do anything right." "You're not good enough." "Nobody loves you." You have power to trade these lies for the truth.

Mirror Confrontation, Mirror Correction

You can't *correct* what you don't *confront*. Only *you* know what lies you believed that wounded your soul. The only thing that cancels a lie is TRUTH! The only thing that can free your soul is TRUTH! Remember this truth: we do not battle with *people,* but rather, with *spirits* (Ephesians 6:12). In this case, it is the *Unloving Spirit* that must be confronted eye to eye. This bully spirit has tormented you long enough. If you have surrendered your life to Jesus' authority, then you have the power of God to take authority over this spirit and bring correction to your thought life! If your mirror has been *cracked,* it's time to restore it *back*!

This confrontation involves a *mirror* and the power of *words*. To sever ties with the Unloving Spirit, you must use a mirror to look closely at yourself in the eye as you state each line of the following declaration. It may help you remember each sentence by first stating it to yourself and then repeating it while looking into a mirror. You should speak in an authoritative tone of voice that empowers you to feel in control. When you're ready . . . look in the mirror and state with confidence:

"Unloving Spirit, I recognize you and expose you as the spirit that has caused me to reject God's love, reject myself, and reject the love of others. Today (date), I dissipate, dismantle, and destroy every lie you ever to sent to make me feel unloved, unwanted, and unworthy! I sever ties with you and no longer give you place to reside in my soul! I fall out of agreement with every word curse that has ever been spoken over my life! I am who GOD says I am! I agree with the truth that I am fearfully and wonderfully made in his image. My identity and my security is deeply rooted and grounded in God's love and acceptance of me just as I am."

Cancel Lies, Declare Truth

As I shared, the only thing that cancels a lie is declaring the truth. Choosing to *fall out of agreement* with the Unloving Spirit gives you power to love who you see in the mirror, as you begin to look at yourself through the filter of *God's love* and *acceptance*.

When you're ready, take a moment to look in the mirror to cancel every lie and declare every new truth you desire to believe about you. Again, if your mirror was cracked, it's time to put it back intact! For example, look in the mirror and declare the following statement. *"Today (date), I cancel the lie that I am worthless! The truth is that my identity is in Christ which gives me worth!"* For each lie you want to cancel, replace it with a new truth. Use this statement as a guide.

To further dismantle the stronghold of the Unloving Spirit, make it a conscious habit to do the following:

1. Practice giving eye contact when speaking to people.
2. When someone gives you a compliment, simply say, "thank you."
3. Avoid criticizing yourself. Instead, practice affirming yourself.
4. Whenever someone wants to bless you in any way, receive it.

I Love What I See When I Look at Me

Imagine how it would honor God (who took the time to design you), to hear you say, *"I love what I see when I look at me."* Our God is the one who "gives life to the dead and calls into being things that were not" (Romans 4:17, NIV). He is your life-giver! You are also to "be renewed in the spirit of your mind" (Ephesians 4:23, KJV). When your *mind* and *spirit* come into agreement, something happens. It's not overnight, but as you make it a habit to say what *God* says about you and *see* what he sees in you, you'll experience a paradigm shift, a transformation in your thinking.

With this transformation, remember these three NEVERS: Never again *loathe* who God *loves*! Never again *criticize* who God *created*! Never again *reject* who God *rejoices* over! Allow only his view to define you!

Mirror Affirmations

The following is a list of daily mirror affirmations that empower you to love and embrace yourself as a creation of God, worthy of love. You can also tailor specific affirmations to fit you.

1. When I look in the mirror, I love what I see. I see a beloved child of God looking back at me.
2. When I look in the mirror, I love what I see. I see a person of worth looking back at me.
3. When I look in the mirror, I love what I see. I see an overcomer looking back at me.
4. When I look in the mirror, I love what I see. I see a magnanimous person looking back at me.
5. When I look in the mirror, I love what I see. I see a person of purpose and destiny looking back at me.
6. When I look in the mirror, I love what I see. I see a person who is fearfully and wonderfully made looking back at me.
7. When I look in the mirror, I love what I see. I see a person who is loved and lovable looking back at me.
8. When I look in the mirror, I love what I see. I see a person who can express love looking back at me.

It is God's will that his truth destroys every lie that has ever affected you. He has the *first* word over you and the *last* word over you! He says in Isaiah 49:16, "See, I have engraved you on the palms of my hands." In Isaiah 43:1 (KJV) the Lord says, "I have redeemed you, I have called you by name, you are mine."

No matter what anyone else has ever called you, God has always called you by your *name* because you belong to him! He declares in Jeremiah 1:5 (NIV), "Before I formed you in the womb I knew you, before you were born I set you apart." Before your mother or father ever knew you, *God* knew you. God has always had intimate knowledge of your life. He knows every abuse, hurt, mistreatment, pain, heartache, sin, and shameful experience you have ever endured.

Four Word Weapon!

When it comes to spoken words, it's not about what someone *calls* you, it's what you *answer* to. It's also not what someone *says* about you, it's whether or not you choose to *receive* it. Years ago, God revealed to me a simple but powerful concept that blocks "deathly" words from entering the spirit. The four word response to any cruel, demeaning, harsh, or hurtful words should be, "I don't receive that!" Looking someone in the eye and making this statement empowers you to immediately reject the spirit of these words from entering *your* spirit! It gives you instant power to *dismantle* and *dissolve* the plot of Satan to wound you! Just because a person says something cruel, harsh, or demeaning doesn't mean you have to receive it. You can choose not to believe it. You can choose not to be hurt. You can choose not to be offended. You have the power to take authority over this plot of Satan by boldly declaring, "I don't receive that!" Believe the truth in 2 Corinthians 10:4 (NKJV), "For the weapons of our warfare are not carnal but mighty in God for pulling down strongholds . . ." This *four word weapon* is powerful and it works! Try it!

God understood the shame and brokenness caused by the treatment of my original first grade teacher. If only I had known to say to her, "I don't receive that!" Yet, in his sovereignty, God used the situation that crushed me as a child to become part of my mission as an adult! That's why he tells us in Isaiah 61:7 (NKJV), "instead of your shame you shall have double honor." I am so thankful God has allowed my life to be poured out as an instrument of hope, healing, and deliverance for countless souls around the world. I never knew that my *brokenness* would one day minister *wholeness*!

Shine for His Glory

The same holds true for you! God will bring good from every moment of shame, guilt, condemnation, sin, abuse, neglect, rejection, hurt, anger, hate, and disappointment you've had in your life! Only God can squeeze *purpose* out of *pain*, *ministry* out of *misery,* and a *message* out of a *mess*! You're still alive because you still have an assignment on the earth. The value of what you've endured and experienced in your life is worth more than a 100-carat diamond. In fact, did you know that a diamond starts out as piece of coal? It's only by intense heating and cutting that a piece of coal produces a shiny diamond. So it is with you. Your painful life experiences will cause you to shine like a diamond for God's glory! Thus, you must "let your light so shine before men, that they may see your good works, and glorify your Father which is in heaven" (Matthew 5:16). This is why choosing to walk in *forgiveness, mercy,* and *love* is so important. It allows you to shine in such a way that your life brings honor to God. Commit to become grounded in the word of God as David did in Psalm 119:11 (NIV) when he wrote "I have hidden your word in my heart so that I will not sin against you." The more you walk in God's ways, the more you'll walk in your worth.

Happy, Healed, and Whole

Matthew 22:37 reminds us to always love God, love you, and love others too. The beginning of all healing and restoration is rooted in developing these three relationships. First and foremost is a right relationship with God. Remember, your identity and security must become so rooted in *God's* love and acceptance that no *person* will ever again have power over you! You are not what anyone else says you are…only what God says you are! Everything he says about you can be found in his 66 books of love letters! Secondly, it's important that you have a right relationship with *yourself*! It's imperative for you to see yourself through God's eyes so you can love yourself as he loves you. There is no one like you! You are a unique, one-of-kind, unrepeatable miracle of God! What I shared earlier bears repeating. Never again *loathe* who God *loves*. Never again *criticize* who God *created*. Never again *reject* who God *rejoices* over. No matter what you've done or what has ever been done to you, you are *loved* and *lovable*! Walking in this truth honors God and liberates you to EMBRACE YOU! Thirdly, healing and restoration begins to flow as you purpose in your heart to have right relationships with *others*. Letting go of hurts from your past and opening your heart to receive love from others will only enrich your life. Remember, peace, joy, good health, and God's favor follow obedience to God's word. That's why choosing to walk in forgiveness, mercy, and love as a *lifestyle* will serve you well for a *lifetime*!

    A *happy* soul is a *healed* soul. A *healed* soul is a *whole* soul. Throughout this book we've been on a journey toward healing and wholeness. I believe practicing the principles shared within these pages will empower you for life. As our journey ends, I have one final word as your "spiritual surgeon" and empowerment coach: *Surgery for the Soul: Healing for the Hurting Heart* was birthed out of *pain* with the *purpose* of divinely giving you a new heart for a new start. Therefore, with your new heart, always allow God's healing power to flow *through* you, so that his amazing love can flow *from* you. Thrust forth!

Surgery for the Soul is an excellent workbooks style reading for bible study groups, women's groups or any small group. Through practical application and thought provoking questions, groups will enjoy taking a journey toward a "new heart" together! To order copies, go to amazon.com.

ABOUT THE AUTHOR

Dr. Brenda L. Caldwell, fondly known as Dr. B, is a premier empowerment speaker, psychologist, forgiveness expert, ordained minister and author. She is a graduate of the University of Memphis and holds a Ph.D. in Christian Psychology. A native of Memphis, TN, she is CEO/Founder of Dr. B Empowerment Services and previously served as empowerment expert for the CBS affiliate Live at 9 Morning Show and the ABC Local Memphis Live Morning Show in Memphis. In October 2015, Dr. Caldwell began a partnership with Jabez House Charity organization in Barbados to provide restoration and healing to women and teen sex workers in need of transformation. She also served five years as a faculty member of the National Youth Professionals Institute in Washington, D.C. Dr. Caldwell is the founder of two award winning empowerment programs for middle school and high school students. She is one of the most versatile presenters in the country, having an ability to connect equally with adult and youth audiences. Dr. Caldwell has been called the "Doctor of Hope" for her unique anointing to deal with "matters of the heart" in a way that makes a profound impact. For over 20 years, she has been in demand as an empowerment speaker, delivering messages of HOPE to thousands of youth, parents, educators, inmates, churches and community organizations across the country and abroad. Dr. Caldwell also possess a very unique ability to teach the "HOW TO" principles of

FORGIVENESS in a way that empowers hurting souls to learn to extend forgiveness as well as to receive forgiveness. In the wake of the eruption of violence, hatred and anger that now spews out across the country, Dr. Caldwell feels called to do her part by presenting the Surgery for the Soul Experience™ to small and large groups throughout the world. Surgery the Soul Experience is a life-changing one day event allowing individuals who are dealing with issues of unforgiveness and other matters of the heart to participate in a unique therapeutic surgery equal to receiving a "new heart!" She conducts customized Surgery for the Soul events for men, women, teens and leaders. For more information or to book Dr. Caldwell for an event, visit www.drbempowers.com

BRENDA L. CALDWELL., PH. D.

REFERENCES

Cohen, E. (2011). Blaming Others can Ruin your Health. *CNN News*. Retrieved on August 25, 2016, from http://www.cnn.com/2011/HEALTH/08/17/bitter.resentful.ep/

Johnson, L. (2015). The Deadly Consequences of Unforgiveness. *CBN News*. Retrieved on August 25, 2016, from
http://www1.cbn.com/cbnnews/healthscience/2015/June/The-Deadly-Consequences-of-Unforgiveness

Linden, M., & Maercker, A. (Eds.). (2011). *Embitterment: Societal, Psychological, and Clinical Perspectives*. Germany: Springer-Verlag Wien.

Nauert PhD, R. (2015). Bitterness Can Make You Sick. *Psych Central*. Retrieved on August 24, 2016, from
http://psychcentral.com/news/2011/08/10/bitterness-can-make-you-sick/28503.html

No Author. (2015). A Heart Surgery Overview. *Texas Heart Institute*. Retrieved on August 26, 2016, from
http://www.texasheart.org/HIC/Topics/Proced/

No Author. (2016). Heart Transplantation. *Montefiore Health System*. Retrieved on August 26, 2016, from http://www.montefiore.org/heart-transplantation

Wrosch, C., & Renaud J. (2011). Self-regulation of bitterness across the lifespan. In Linden, M., &

Maercker, A. (Eds.), *Embitterment: Societal, Psychological, and Clinical Perspectives* (pp. 129-141). Germany: Springer-Verlag Wien.

CONTACT INFORMATION

To Book Dr. Brenda L. Caldwell for the following adult or youth related events, go to www.drbempowers.com or call 662-775-0538.

Surgery for the Soul Experience™: Featuring *The Forgiveness Wall*, Surgery for the Soul Experience is a highly impactful one-day experiential experience that first teaches the biblical principles of forgiveness and then engages participants in an unforgettable life altering therapeutic forgiveness "surgery" that frees the soul! Participants learn the "how to" principles of *extending* forgiveness as well as *receiving* forgiveness. This engaging, eye opening experience empowers individuals to receive a "new heart for a new start." Due to the increase of unhealed hurt throughout the world, Surgery for the Soul Experience™ remains in high demand!

Dr. Caldwell presents four customized Surgery for the Soul events to accommodate specific audience needs.

*Surgery for the Soul Experience for Men™

*Surgery for the Soul Experience for Women™

*Surgery for the Soul Experience for Teens™

BRENDA L. CALDWELL., PH. D.

*Surgery for the Soul Experience for Leaders™

Church Services: As an ordained minister and evangelist, Dr. Caldwell speaks at church events for men, women, youth, singles as well as for families. Sought after for her unique experiential style, she delivers anointed transformative truth that ignites lasting change as a vessel of God.

Women's Ministry: Dr. Caldwell delivers anointed, interactive keynotes, retreats, workshops and special events that address women's issues in a way that yields healing, deliverance and wholeness. She has a unique anointing that empowers women to discover their true worth, purpose and potential.

Singles Ministry: Dr. Caldwell delivers anointed, interactive keynotes, retreats, workshops and special events that address the issues of singles who are divorced, widowed or those who have never married. As a happy and whole single, she ministers from experience to help other singles embrace their singleness as a gift.

The Blessing Ceremony: The Blessing Ceremony is a

60-90 minute special ceremony conducted corporately for churches or for individual families desiring to release a biblical blessing upon loved ones that empowers him or her to prosper in every area of life (spiritually, mentally, emotionally, financially, economically and socially). This is a ceremony that also strengthens the bond and relationships of family members.

Empowerment Coaching/Counseling:

Dr. Caldwell provides one-on-one coaching and worldwide counseling services to promote positive change in clients. Specializing in matters of the heart, she conducts individual and family sessions to affectively address root issues. Dr. Caldwell uses spiritual and practical principles to empower clients to overcome areas of past hurts that may be hindering clients from achieving their goals. She is known for her ability to provide results oriented "how to" steps to enable clients to overcome personal obstacles in pursuit of healing and restoration.

Keynote Speaking:

Dr. Caldwell is a highly requested keynote speaker for conferences, summits, banquets and retreats. Her presence is highly regarded because of her distinctive style that is authentic, alive, thought provoking, compassionate and humorous. She possesses an anointing that captivates and grabs the hearts of audiences from all walks of life.

"There is one ingredient I must have to ensure the success of all my conferences...Dr. B! Enough said."
Darrell B. Daniels, Conference Planner, Tampa, FL

Youth Assemblies: Dr. Caldwell partners with middle schools, high schools and youth organizations to provide thought provoking, life altering assembly programs and motivational events to thousands of students each year.

Diplomas Count!™ Assembly Program:

Diplomas Count! is a 90 minute life altering experiential assembly program that ignites hope in the hearts of high school students! It not only addresses the root causes of dropping out, but through engaging and experiential activities, students experience an epiphany that makes them more determined to graduate than ever!

Bully Busters™ Assembly Program:

Bully Busters is a 90 minute assembly program designed to equip middle school and high school students to effectively address issues of bullying with courage and confidence. Through Dr. Caldwell's unusual ability to connect with the toughest students, bullies often seek to make amends after participating in this experiential assembly that exposes the root causes and effects of bullying.

Diamond Girls™ Assembly Program:

Diamond Girls is a 90 minute assembly program designed to empower and inspire female middle school and high schools to develop healthy self esteem, self worth and healthy peer relationships. In this engaging, experiential and energetic program, female students learn to embrace their commonalities and differences in a way that helps to ignite a change in the culture of the school amongst girls.

DreamReachers™ Assembly Program:

DreamReachers Assembly Program for middle school and high school students, is a high energy, thought provoking assembly program that empowers and inspires students to make right choices in order to fulfill their dreams.

BRENDA L. CALDWELL., PH. D.

"Uncommon. Rare. Exceptional. Inspirational. Motivational. Electrifying. Each word describes Dr. B! Throughout my tenure as a principal, I have never met a speaker who possesses the charisma and innate ability to instill hope in the lives of students. Her ability to connect with students is phenomenal!"

Abby Robinson, Retired Principal, Forrest City High School-Forrest City, AR

Educational Consulting:

Dr. Caldwell provides culture change consulting to schools as well as in-service training and motivational workshops to empower and inspire educators and faculty members in their work with students. In fact, her events for educators and youth professionals are equal to a B12 shot!

"Within our cadre of experts, Dr. Caldwell stands out because she is imbued with a spirit that is truly awe-inspiring!"

J. Tyler-Vice President of Training Services, WAVE, Incorporated-Washington, D.C.

Discover the power of your words, your impact, and the greatness that only you offer!

From Charcoal to Diamond: Discover the Greatness in You, is a powerfully uplifting, inspiring, and informative book by Dr. Brenda Caldwell that offers remarkable insight into the transformation of a piece of coal into a sparkling diamond, relating it to your own life.

This interactive book is purposefully compact and power-packed to make an impact on your life as you uncover the secrets to maximizing the real greatness within you. Wherever you are in life, this book will empower you to realize your true value, worth, and potential! **Purchase at Amazon.com or go to www.drbempowers.com**

www.ingramcontent.com/pod-product-compliance
Lightning Source LLC
Chambersburg PA
CBHW070453100426
42743CB00010B/1595